Asia's Masonic Reformation

FREEMASONRY'S IMPACT ON THE
WESTERNIZATION AND SUBSEQUENT
MODERNIZATION OF ASIA

Kristine Ohkubo
(SECOND EDITION)

Copyright © 2023 by Kristine Ohkubo.

All rights reserved. No part of this publication may be reproduced, distributed or transmitted in any form or by any means, including photocopying, recording, or other electronic or mechanical methods, without the prior written permission of the author, except in the case of brief quotations embodied in critical reviews and certain other noncommercial uses permitted by copyright law. For permission requests, contact the author using the website address provided below.

https://kristineohkubo.wixsite.com/nonfiction-author

Asia's Masonic Reformation/Kristine Ohkubo. —2nd ed.

ISBN 978-0578447308

CONTENTS

Introduction 1
The Theoretical History of the Craft 4
    The Stonemasons 5
    The Accepted or Gentleman Masons 6
    The Mystery Religions 8
    The Pythagorean Brotherhood 9
    The Triangle in Masonic Symbolism 13
    The Legend of Hiram Abiff 15
    The Knights Templar 19
    The Knights Hospitaller 20
    Rosicrucianism 21
    Order of the Golden Dawn 22
Tenets of Freemasonry 25
The Degrees of Freemasonry 29
Key Dates Pertaining to the Emergence and Spread of Freemasonry in Europe and America 34
Freemasonry Proliferates in Europe and America 38
    France 42
    Italy 43
    Germany 43
    Russia 46
    North America 46

Mexico 48

The Gormogons 50

Key Dates in Chinese History 51

Confucianism, Taoism, and Freemasonry 54

Freemasonry Reaches China 59

The Chinese Freemasons 64

Sun Yat-sen 67

Situ Meitang 74

The End of the Qing Dynasty 81

The Post-Revolution Chinese Freemasons 84

The Triads and the Umbrella Revolution 88

Freemasonry in Communist China 90

Key Dates in Japanese History 93

Bushido, Shinto, and Freemasonry 98

Freemasonry Gains a Foothold in Japan 104

Isaac Titsingh 105

Commodore Matthew C. Perry 106

Thomas Blake Glover 110

John Fulton Calder 121

The Freemasons in Yokohama 122

The First Japanese Freemasons 123

The Anti-Masonic Movement 132

Judaic-Masonic Conspiracy Theories 133

General Douglas MacArthur	136
Freemasonry Returns	140
Attempts to Suppress Freemasonry	152
Freemasons versus Shriners	171
Glossary of Masonic Terms	181
List of Photos and Illustrations	189
Works Cited	196
About the Author	207

"All conspiracy theories are the product of the subconscious attempt of an ignorant yet creative mind to counteract the fear of the unknown with tales of fantasy."

―*Abhijit Naskar*

"Great men do not become Freemasons by the virtue of their greatness, they are great men because they are Freemasons."

—*Master Mason, 33rd Degree*

INTRODUCTION

Shrouded by mystery, misinformation, and conspiracy, Freemasonry remains one of the least understood organizations of all time. It appears incomprehensible to most people because it contains a constantly evolving and adapting ideology defined by a commitment to universal brotherhood and self-improvement. Freemasonry is not governed by a single governing body but is made up of a loose network of groups, known as lodges, that fall under the jurisdiction of regional and national grand lodges.

As of this writing, the brotherhood consists of over six million members worldwide and has included some of the most powerful men in history.[1] While Freemasonry has enjoyed unprecedented growth since its development in the 18th century, it still remains inaccessible to women (although other corresponding bodies, such as the Order of the Eastern Star, admit women who are wives and female relatives of Freemasons).

Two common beliefs endure among all Freemasons. The first is that each man has a responsibility to improve himself while being devoted to his family, country, and fraternity. The second is that each man has

---

[1] "Welcome to UGLE, 2018." United Grand Lodge of England.
www.ugle.org.uk/about-freemasonry/frequently-asked-questions.

a responsibility to help make the world a better place. These beliefs have been the basis which have enabled Freemasons to be catalysts for change throughout history.

As Western culture and influence penetrated the far corners of the world, Freemasons were notably at the forefront, ushering in rapid change, modernization, and enlightenment. Was this merely coincidental, or was it by design?

I invite you to follow along and reach your own conclusion as I present you with details and irrefutable historical facts demonstrating how the West has had a profound influence on the collective and diverse customs and traditions maintained by the numerous ethnic groups of Asia. It is undeniable that where the West has left its footprints on the sands of time, the Freemasons have often had a presence.

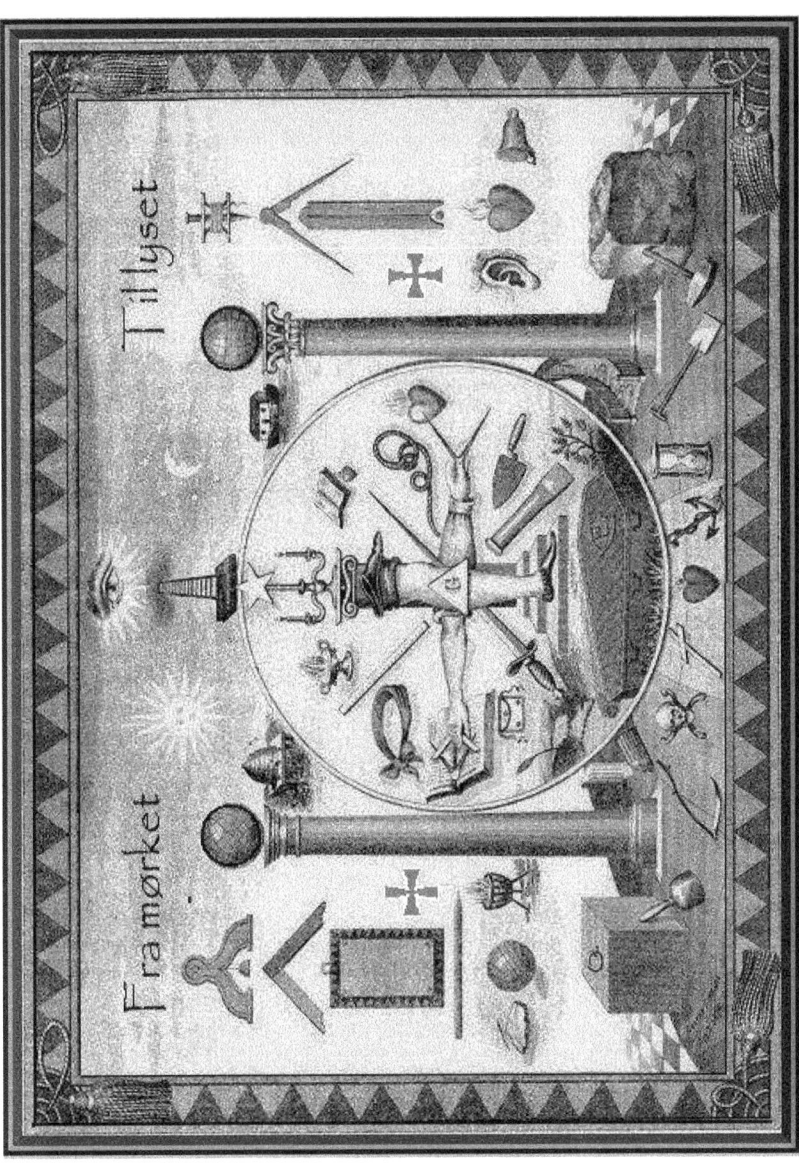

1. Alle Frimurer Symboler

CHAPTER 1

The Theoretical History of the Craft

Over the years there have been numerous attempts to trace back the evolution of the secretive Masonic fraternity. Several historians and scholars, both Masons and non-Masons, have claimed that Freemasonry owes its roots to the Greco-Roman mysteries. Other theories allege that Freemasonry was derived from the Egyptian pyramid builders or the bands of traveling stonemasons acting under Papal authority. Further speculation suggests that Freemasonry was in existence when King Solomon built the Temple at Jerusalem. The stonemasons who built the temple were organized into lodges and allegedly, Hiram Abiff, the chief architect of the temple, served as the Master Mason. Freemasonry has also been linked to the Knights Templar who supposedly escaped to Scotland after the order was persecuted in Europe. Some historians have gone so far as to claim Freemasonry owes its past to the Rosicrucian Brotherhood.

The fact remains there is very little written evidence to draw upon when investigating the origin of Freemasonry. The oldest document in existence which makes reference to the Freemasons is the *Halliwell Manuscript*, also known as the *Regius Poem* (circa 1390).[2] The document was discovered in the British Museum by James Halliwell in 1838 and recounts how the craft of Freemasonry was brought to England during the reign of King Athelstan, the first king of England, who reigned from 924 to 939.[3] In fact, it wasn't until four lodges in London came together and formed a Grand Lodge in June of 1717, that more complete records on Freemasonry emerged.

While it is true that modern Freemasonry bears some similarity to ancient organizations by way of their initiation rituals, symbolism, and philosophy, there really is no substantiating proof that it is directly related to any of them. It is far more likely that Freemasonry has borrowed and adapted elements from these ancient orders as well as other social influences to create the Freemasonry of today. No evidence has ever been presented that specifically connects Freemasonry to any ancient origin. However, in order to understand the basis for these theories, it is necessary to examine, at least cursorily, these ancient customs and organizations.

The Stonemasons

Among the various theories which exist the most widely accepted is that Freemasonry evolved from the countless stonemasons' guilds that existed during the Middle Ages. These medieval stonemasons (or operative masons) built the great cathedrals and castles of the

---

[2] "Masonic Manuscripts." Wikipedia. Wikimedia Foundation.
https://en.wikipedia.org/wiki/Masonic_manuscripts.
[3] "Æthelstan." Wikipedia. Wikimedia Foundation.
https://en.wikipedia.org/wiki/%C3%86thelstan.

time. They were known to gather in lodges to rest and eat, and gradually these lodges became places where the stonemasons could regulate their craft. With this development, initiation ceremonies for new apprentices were adopted.

The stonemasons traveled all over the country from one building site to another and began using a secret code word to prove that the individual was properly trained and had been a member of a lodge.[4]

The Accepted or Gentleman Masons

In the early 1600s, these operative lodges began to admit men who had no connection with the trade. These new members came to be known as *accepted* or *gentlemen Masons*. Shortly thereafter, Freemasonry spread rapidly throughout Europe and the American colonies. George Washington (*initiated in Fredericksburg, Virginia, and Past Master of Alexandria Lodge No. 22, Virginia*), Benjamin Franklin (*initiated at St. John's Lodge, Philadelphia, February 1731 and made Grand Master in 1734*), Paul Revere (*initiated at St. Andrew's Lodge, Boston, Massachusetts, September 1760 and served nine terms as Worshipful Master, five with St. Andrew's Lodge and four with Rising States Lodge, Massachusetts*), Joseph Warren (*Lodge of Saint Andrew in Boston*), and John Paul Jones (*St. Bernard's Lodge No. 122, Kirkcudbright, Scotland*) were all Freemasons.[5]

---

[4] "History of Freemasonry." Wikipedia. Wikimedia Foundation. https://en.wikipedia.org/wiki/History_of_Freemasonry.
[5] "Freemasonry of Massachusetts." Paul Revere Lodge of Freemasons. https://paulreverelodge.org.

During the late 1700s, the fraternity was deeply involved in spreading what was referred to as the "ideals of the enlightenment."[6] These ideals focused on the dignity of man, the liberty of the individual, the right of all persons to worship as they choose, the formation of democratic governments, and the importance of public education.

Freemasonry grew dramatically during the 1800s and early 1900s. At that time a social safety net did not exist, so anyone falling ill or becoming disabled had to rely on friends and the English Poor Law for support (Early American policies for publicly funded poor relief were patterned after the English Poor Laws.). It was during this time when the Freemasons engaged in founding orphanages, homes for widows, and homes for the elderly.

Today, the brotherhood continues to participate in various charitable and philanthropic activities. Although some activities are well known and publicized, the majority of its charitable work is performed privately, without widespread public knowledge.[7]

Having covered the evolution of Freemasonry from the point of view of the more generally accepted theory, let's examine its other, more spiritual and secretive aspects. For instance, why have historians and scholars so often attributed the basis of Freemasonry's secret initiation rituals to the religious schools of the Greco-Roman world?

---

[6] "Who Are the Freemason?" Be a Shriner Now.
www.beashrinernow.com/About/Freemasons/AboutFreemasons.
[7] "History of Freemasonry." Wikipedia.

The Mystery Religions

The mystery religions, which flourished in late antiquity, faced persecution from the Christian Roman Empire and therefore maintained an element of secrecy with regard to their initiation rites, ritual practices, and beliefs.

The Mysteries schools, which included the Eleusinian Mysteries, the Dionysian Mysteries, and the Orphic Mysteries incorporated certain aspects of the polytheistic Indo-European religion, and thus stood in direct contrast to the monotheistic teachings of Christianity.

The word "mystery" is derived from the Greek verb "myein," which means to close (referring to the lips and the eyes). The Mysteries were secret cults into which a person had to be initiated. There were certain integral features which strengthened the bonds of each cult such as common meals, dances, ceremonies, and particularly initiation rites.[8]

There were no written records revealing the essence of these Mysteries. Their meaning was only revealed to the initiates during the festivals, making it impossible for the non-initiated to gain insight into the secret cults. Furthermore, it was considered a treachery to reveal the secret dances to the outsiders.

In time, some of these secret societies dropped their religious connections and merely became social clubs. However, since

---

[8] "Mystery religion: Greco-Roman religion." Encyclopedia Britannica. https://www.britannica.com/topic/mystery-religion.

secrecy, common meals, and common drinking were still maintained, the Greeks and Romans regarded such clubs as Mystery societies; they did not differentiate between religious associations and private clubs.

In addition to secrecy, other elements of the Mysteries schools are commonly believed to have been incorporated into the Masonic fraternity. Among these are the spiritual traditions of Freemasonry and the use of symbolism.

Unlike the Dionysian Mysteries, the Orphic Mysteries centered on the creation myth. Behind the myth is the religion of salvation for the human soul. The Orphic cult was heavily influenced by Eastern beliefs, particularly with regard to the transmigration of the soul, and the incorporation of guilt and sins.[9] To the Orphic followers, the physical body was merely a prison or tomb for the soul. They believed that by living an austere and virtuous life and ridding oneself of evil they would be rewarded in the afterlife.[10]

The Pythagorean Brotherhood

The Orphic creeds were the basis of the Pythagorean brotherhood, which flourished in southern Italy during the 6th century. The brotherhood was an aristocratic fraternity capable of wielding political power. Influenced by mathematics and mysticism, they invested music, geometry, and astronomy with religious values.

---

[9] "Proto-Indo-Iranian religion." Wikipedia. Wikimedia Foundation. https://en.wikipedia.org/wiki/Proto-Indo-Iranian_religion.
[10] "Greco-Roman Mysteries." Wikipedia. Wikimedia Foundation. https://en.wikipedia.org/wiki/Greco-Roman_mysteries.

ii. Statue of George Washington in Masonic garb at the Masonic Hall in New York City

iii. Benjamin Franklin Opening the Lodge (Published by Kurz and Allison of Chicago, 1896)

According to their doctrine the soul originally resided in the stars before it fell down to earth and associated with the body. Thus, man's mission was to liberate himself from the ties of the flesh and return to the soul's celestial home.

Candidates for the Pythagorean brotherhood underwent a secret initiation process and swore an oath of the tetractys (mystic triangle). Upon initiation the novices also took a five-year vow of silence.

The tetractys was a mystic symbol and very important to Pythagoreanism. The symbol consisted of a triangular figure composed of ten points arranged in four rows. The number four was significant as it was associated with the four seasons, planetary motions, and music.[11]

One of the most noted Pythagoreans was Florence-born Arturo Reghini, a writer, translator, and mathematician. He started his Masonic career in 1902, while he was simultaneously receiving instruction on the Pythagorean tradition. Reghini was initiated into the Order of Memphis and Misraim, which incorporated the myths and symbols from ancient Egypt into its rites.[12]

---

[11] "Tetractys." Wikipedia. Wikimedia Foundation. https://en.wikipedia.org/wiki/Tetractys.
[12] "Secular Mystery Communities." Encyclopædia Britannica. Encyclopædia Britannica, Inc. https://www.britannica.com/topic/mystery-religion/Secular-mystery-communities.

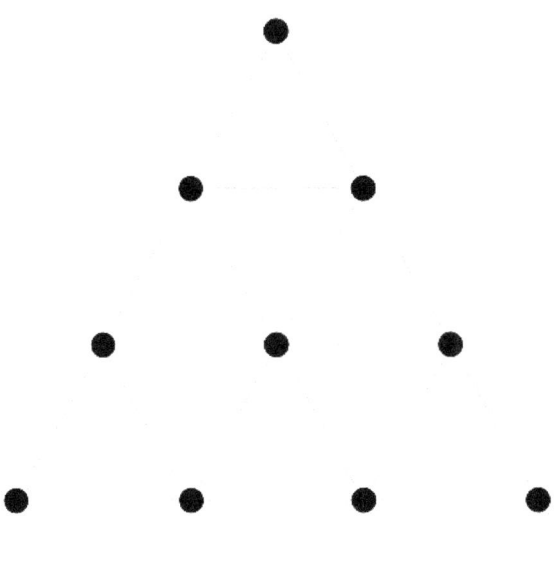

iv. Pythagorean tetractys

The Triangle in Masonic Symbolism

The triangle also holds an important place in Masonic symbolism. The equilateral triangle, a triangle of three equal sides and equal angles, was used by nearly all of the ancient civilizations as a symbol of their deity. To the Egyptians, this triangle hieroglyphically symbolized the trowel and served as an important tool for the operative Mason. The triangle is said to symbolically connect and bond Freemasons with each other and with their deity. The triangle is also used to enclose another Masonic symbol known as the Eye of Providence, or the all-seeing eye of God. It first appeared as the standard iconography of the Freemasons in 1797 in a publication entitled *Freemasons Monitor or Illustrations of Masonry: In Two Parts* by Thomas Smith Webb. Webb, who was born in Massachusetts in 1771, became a Freemason in 1790 at the

Rising Sun Lodge and went on to become a prominent ritualist and lecturer.[13] Freemasons refer to God as the Great Architect of the Universe and the all-seeing eye is a reminder that man's thoughts and deeds are always observed.

The Great Seal of the United States incorporates the Eye of Providence atop an unfinished pyramid, but many Masonic organizations have explicitly denied any connection with the creation of the seal.[14]

The pyramids themselves are a source of mystery and have resulted in many diverse theories over time. It was previously believed that the ancient Egyptian pyramids were constructed by slave laborers numbering a hundred thousand according to Greek historian Herodotus' account. This idea was further perpetuated by Hollywood in such films as *The Ten Commandments*, but relatively recent research conducted by renown Egyptologists Mark Lehner and Zahi Hawaas indicates that the pyramids were built by an organized, rotating labor force of twenty to thirty thousand. In fact, the Great Pyramid of Giza, which was constructed during the 4th century, is believed to have been built by a skeleton crew of workers who labored year-round and were joined by farmers and villagers from the

---

[13] "Thomas Smith Webb." Wikipedia. Wikimedia Foundation. https://en.wikipedia.org/wiki/Thomas_Smith_Webb.
[14] "The Equilateral Triangle." The Grand Lodge of Texas. The Masonic Trowel.com. http://www.themasonictrowel.com/Articles/degrees/degree_3rd_files/theequilateral_triangle_gltx.htm.

v. The Eye of Providence as seen on the U.S. $1 bill

surrounding areas in late summer and early autumn when the Nile River flooded. This theory would give credence to the idea that Freemasonry was derived from the Egyptian pyramid builders, but there is no substantiating proof.[15]

The Legend of Hiram Abiff

The legend of Hiram Abiff is conveyed to all Freemasons during the third degree. Hiram's true identity is uncertain, but the name does appear in the Bible's *Old Testament*. In 2 Samuel 5:11 and 1 Kings 5:1-10, Hiram is the King of Tyre (Lebanon), and is credited with having sent building materials and men for the construction of the

---

[15] "Who Built the Pyramids?" Nova. http://www.pbs.org/wgbh/nova/ancient/who-built-the-pyramids.html

Temple in Jerusalem. The passages below are taken from the King James version.

> *And Hiram king of Tyre sent messengers to David, and cedar trees, and carpenters, and masons: and they built David an house. (2 Samuel 5:11)*

Then in 1 Kings 5:1-10, it states:

> *And Hiram king of Tyre sent his servants unto Solomon; for he had heard that they had anointed him king in the room of his father: for Hiram was ever a lover of David.*

> *And Hiram sent to Solomon, saying, I have considered the things which thou sentest to me for: and I will do all thy desire concerning timber of cedar, and concerning timber of fir.*

> *My servants shall bring them down from Lebanon unto the sea: and I will convey them by sea in floats unto the place that thou shalt appoint me, and will cause them to be discharged there, and thou shalt receive them: and thou shalt accomplish my desire, in giving food for my household.*

> *So Hiram gave Solomon cedar trees and fir trees according to all his desire.*

In 1 Kings 7:13–14, Hiram is the son of a widow from the tribe of Naphtali, who was sent for by Solomon to cast the bronze furnishings and ornate decorations for the new temple.

Now King Solomon sent and brought Huram from Tyre.

He was the son of a widow from the tribe of Naphtali, and his father was a man of Tyre, a bronze worker; he was filled with wisdom and understanding and skill in working with all kinds of bronze work. So he came to King Solomon and did all his work.

According to the tale passed down in Masonic lodges, Hiram was appointment by Solomon as chief architect or Master Mason. He was ambushed by three stonemasons as the temple was nearing completion and challenged to divulge the secrets of a Master Mason, the revelation of which would have enabled them to earn higher wages. Hiram refused and was struck dead with a stonemason's tool. His body was buried in a shallow grave only to be discovered by other stonemasons the next day. Hiram was given a proper burial and the secrets of the Master Masons were allegedly buried along with the body.

Today, during lodge meetings, tradition dictates that the Deputy Grand Master be seated to the left of the Grand Master in what is called the Chair of Hiram Abiff.[16]

---

[16] "Hiram Abiff." Wikipedia. Wikimedia Foundation. https://en.wikipedia.org/wiki/Hiram_Abiff.

vi. Masonic Third Degree Tracing Board [17] showing Hiram Abiff in his coffin by unknown artist, (Circa 1830s) from the Museum of Freemasonry

---

[17] *Tracing boards are painted or printed illustrations depicting the various emblems and symbols of Freemasonry. They can be used as teaching aids during the lectures that follow each of the Masonic Degrees, when an experienced member explains the various concepts of Freemasonry to new members. They can also be used by experienced members as reminders of the concepts they learned as they went through the ceremonies of the different Masonic degrees.*

The Knights Templar

In 1737 Chevalier Andrew Michael Ramsay, a Scottish-born writer who lived in France, published the *Discourse pronounced at the reception of Freemasons by Monsieur de Ramsay, Grand Orator of the Order*, suggesting that the Freemasons were closely connected to the Knights Templar. It did not include supporting evidence to his claim, but it created a huge wave of interest in Freemasonry at the time. Also, it generated a strong desire among Freemasons to participate in knightly orders.

There were several unsuccessful attempts to legitimize the claim. Those who attempted to make the connection between the Knights Templar and the Freemasons alleged that the Templars escaped to Scotland in 1307 after being persecuted by King Philip of France and Pope Clement V. They further claimed that the Templars aided Robert the Bruce in winning Scotland's first war of independence against England in 1314. However, there was never any conclusive evidence showing that there were any Templar Knights on the battlefield during the Battle of Bannockburn.

There are some who contend that when Ramsay wrote, "Our ancestors, the Crusaders, gathered together from all parts of Christendom in the Holy Land, desired thus to reunite into one sole Fraternity the individuals of all nations," he was referring to the Knights Hospitaller and not the Knights Templar.[18]

---

[18] "Knights Templar Discoveries." KnightsTemplarFreemasonry.com. http://www.knightstemplarfreemasonry.com/templar_freemasonry_connection.htm.

The Knights Hospitaller

vii. The Knights Hospitaller in the 13th century

The Knights Hospitaller, also known as the Order of Saint John, were a medieval Catholic military order that became the modern Sovereign Military Order of Malta. They were headquartered in Jerusalem, the island of Rhodes, Malta, and Rome. They, along with the Knights Templar grew into the most formidable military orders in the Holy Land.

Today, there exists a Masonic order known as the Knights Templar. It consists of Freemasons in good standing who have been through the degrees of the Holy Royal Arch. Founded in 1895, they are officially known as the United Religious, Military and Masonic Orders of the Temple and of St John of Jerusalem, Palestine, Rhodes, and Malta of England and Wales and its Provinces Overseas. They base their Masonic iconography on the historic crusading orders, the Knights Templar and the Knights Hospitaller, but bare no direct lineal connection to the historical military orders from which they derive their name.[19]

Rosicrucianism

Rosicrucianism was a cultural movement which arose in Europe in the early 17th century after the publication of several texts which claimed the existence of certain esoteric truths from the ancient past pertaining to nature, the physical universe, and the spiritual realm. These manifestos combined the concepts of Kabbalah, Hermeticism, Alchemy and mystical Christianity, and heralded the universal reformation of mankind. They also alluded to the existence of a secret brotherhood of alchemists and sages who were preparing to transform the arts, sciences, religion, and political and intellectual landscapes of Europe.

The goal of the Rosicrucians was to throw occult light upon the misunderstood Christian religion and to explain the mystery of life and being from the scientific standpoint in harmony with religion. Rosicrucianism had a considerable influence on Anglo-Saxon Freemasonry.[20]

Toward the end of the 18th century, two Rosicrucian-inspired Masonic rites emerged—the Rectified Scottish Rite and the Ancient

---

[19] Cartwright, Mark. "Knights Hospitaller." World History Encyclopedia. https://www.worldhistory.org/Knights_Hospitaller/.
[20] "Rosicrucianism." TheosophyWiki. http://theosophy.wiki/w-en/index.php?title=Rosicrucianism.

viii. A piece of jewelry of the "18° Knight of the Rose Croix" Scottish Rite (20th century image)

and Accepted Scottish Rite. The first rite became widespread in Central Europe, while the second was initially practiced in France. The Ancient and Accepted Scottish Rite's 18th degree is called Knight of the Rose Croix. [21]

Order of the Golden Dawn

In 1888, a secret fraternal organization was founded by Dr. William Wescott, a physician, coroner, and part-time occultist. Known as the Order of the Golden Dawn, its members were devoted to the study

---

[21] "Rosicrucianism." Wikipedia. Wikimedia Foundation. https://en.wikipedia.org/wiki/Rosicrucianism.

and practice of the occult, metaphysics, and paranormal activities during the late 19th and early 20th centuries. The Order drew heavily on the tradition of Victorian Freemasonry and the Rosicrucian movement, but was not an augmentation of either. It was a true secret society, marked by strong hierarchical and ritualistic systems. Victorian Freemasonry was far more concerned with esoteric and occult matters than the mainstream craft. The Order also distinguished itself from its Masonic predecessors through the inclusion of women, who were admitted on an equal basis with men.[22]

******

The origin and evolution of Freemasonry will more than likely be debated for many years to come, but through examining the various known elements of symbolism, ceremony, and initiation, we can at least gain some understanding of the various theories that have emerged through the years—theories that in the opinion of this author can be dismissed on the basis that they do not enlighten one with the knowledge of the true purpose and intent of Freemasonry as an organization. Furthermore, the very nature of the fraternity—which emphasizes secrecy—will undoubtedly trigger other theories to crop up over time, some even pointing to conspiracy, but always offering very little insight into the actual objectives of the brotherhood. The matter is further complicated by the emergence of non-sanctioned lodges whose principles deviate from the fundamental and primary

---

[22] "Hermetic Order of the Golden Dawn." Wikipedia. Wikimedia Foundation. https://en.wikipedia.org/wiki/Hermetic_Order_of_the_Golden_Dawn.

doctrines and philosophies of the established and sanctioned Masonic lodges.

ix. Freemasonry emblem -the masonic square and compass symbol

The letter "G" in the center has multiple meanings depending on the context in which it is discussed. In certain instances the letter "G" represents Geometry "the basis upon which the superstructure of Freemasonry, and everything in existence in the entire universe is erected." In other instances it stands for the Great Architect of the Universe (a non-denominational reference to God).[23]

---

[23] "Square and Compasses." Wikipedia. Wikimedia Foundation. https://en.wikipedia.org/wiki/Square_and_Compasses.

CHAPTER 2

Tenets of Freemasonry

Freemasons have a set of basic ethical principles that they all live by. These principles are known as the "Tenets of Freemasonry" and consist of brotherly love, relief, and truth. A tenet by definition is a principle, belief, or doctrine generally held to be true, particularly one that is held in common by members of an organization, movement, or profession.[24] In Freemasonry, the three principles are not just a series of commonly held beliefs; they form the foundation on which the fraternity was created.

1. **Brotherly love**: denotes a relationship of deep compassion, affection, and understanding. To have brotherly love for someone implies that the person is truly cared for and valued as an individual, in the same manner a member of someone's own family would be.

---

[24] "Definition of tenet." Merriam-Webster Online. https://www.merriam-webster.com/dictionary/tenet.

2. **Relief:** signifies the removal of or the unburdening from something oppressive, painful, or distressing. In the Masonic definition, it refers to genuinely caring about each other's welfare and strengthening the bond with one another.

3. **Truth:** can be defined as sincerity in action, character, and expression. A Mason's words, actions, and character should be one of integrity, embodying both the highest standards of morality and the image of the Creator.

In addition to the three tenets mentioned above there are four cardinal virtues which form the "Seven Moral Principles of Freemasonry." The four virtues consist of temperance, fortitude, prudence, and justice. These virtues have long been recognized in classical antiquity and in traditional Christian theology.

1. **Temperance**: is often understood to imply restraint, practice of self-control, abstention, discretion, and moderation.

2. **Fortitude**: is defined as courage, strength, endurance, and ability to confront fear, uncertainty, and intimidation.

3. **Prudence**: is the ability to judge between choices of action with regard to taking appropriate actions at a given time.

4. **Justice:** implies fairness and is considered perhaps the most extensive and most important virtue. The Greek word from which it is derived also means righteousness.[25]

These ethical principles and cardinal virtues are the factors by which all Freemasons are judged when a determination is made with regard to whether the members are in *good standing*.

Generally, a person cannot become a Freemason simply by request. Candidates for Freemasonry are usually observed for a period of time prior to being invited to a lodge social function, or some form of open evening at the lodge. The potential Freemason will attend accompanied by a sponsor. Sponsorship carries with it a great deal of responsibility, and the potential sponsor must think matters through very carefully before accepting this role. A sponsor is ultimately held responsible for anything the candidate may say or do, thus damaging the sponsor's own standing with the lodge if anything does go wrong. Afterwards, the candidate must meet the most active members of the lodge and submit to an interview process through which the candidate's suitability for membership is determined. If the candidate successfully passes the interview process, there will be a lodge vote to determine whether he is accepted.

---

[25] Addison II, L.C. "The Tenets of Freemasonry: Mere Words or Good Guidelines?" Grand Lodge of Iowa.org.
http://grandlodgeofiowa.org/docs/Philosophy_Masonry/TheTenetsofFreemasonry.pdf.

The absolute minimum requirement is that the candidate be free and of good character. The requirement to be free simply implies that the candidate must be willing to join the fraternity on his own accord. There is an unwritten but universally understood rule that no Mason shall ask his friend to join the brotherhood.[26] Most grand lodges require that the candidate declare a belief in a supreme being. In Continental Freemasonry, exemplified by the Grand Orient de France, however, it is not a requirement to declare a belief in any deity. This has caused friction with the rest of Freemasonry as the Grand Orient accepts atheists.

During the ceremony of initiation the candidate is expected to place his hand on a Bible and swear an oath to fulfil certain obligations as a Freemason. In the course of completing the three degrees, new Freemasons will make two promises: to keep the knowledge they gained as part of their degree secret from lower degree Freemasons and outsiders, and to support a fellow Freemason in distress (as far as practicality and the law permits). Instruction is given as to the duties of a Freemason, but on the whole Freemasons are left to explore the craft in the manner they find most satisfying. Some members will further explore the rituals and symbolism of the craft, others will focus their involvement on the social aspects of the lodge, while others will concentrate on the charitable functions of the lodge.

---

[26] Mathews, John T. "The Candidate." Masonic Relief, Charity and You. Masonic World. www.masonicworld.com/education/files/artnov01/The%20Candidate.htm.

CHAPTER 3

The Degrees of Freemasonry

*"The word **degree**, in its primitive meaning, signifies a step. The degrees of Freemasonry are, then, the steps by which the candidate ascends from a lower to a higher condition of knowledge."*

~Albert G. Mackey

The Encyclopedia of Freemasonry, 1873

If we are to accept the dogma that Freemasonry arose from the Egyptian pyramid builders or the bands of traveling stonemasons in Europe, we can ascertain that the degrees of Freemasonry retain the three grades of the craft guilds: *Apprentice* (Entered Apprentice), *Journeyman* or *Fellow* (Fellowcraft), and *Master Mason*.

The candidate members of these three degrees are progressively taught the meanings of the symbols of Freemasonry and entrusted with grips, signs, and words to signify to other members that they have been so initiated.

Within the Masonic membership, the highest rank that can be attained is that of Master Mason. The other degrees which are obtained through passage into other rites are called *appendant degrees.* These appendant degrees are lateral movements within the highest degree of Master Mason (third degree). The appendant degrees differ based upon which rite the Master Mason participates in.

The appendant degrees are not a ranking system but rather an honorary title. Masons that are so designated are simply being acknowledged for conducting themselves in an enhanced manner within the designation of Master Mason. For example, a Master Mason raised to the 33rd degree does not rank above a Master Mason raised to the 32nd degree. These levels merely signify advancement through a set of core principles within different rites.

The Scottish Rite has 33 appendant degrees, whereas the York Rite has 32. A Master Mason who has been raised to the 33rd degree with the Scottish Rite does not outrank a Master Mason who has obtained the 32nd degree in the York Rite. As a matter of fact, every member is afforded the same level of respect within the brotherhood whether they are an Entered Apprentice, Fellowcraft, or Master Mason.

However, respect does not necessarily translate into rights. There is a hierarchy when it comes to the three degrees of Freemasonry in which rights come into play. For example, those Masons who have only completed the first degree are eligible to attend only the meetings involving matters pertaining to the first degree. Those who have been raised to the second degree can attend meetings intended for those who have completed the first and second degrees. Master Masons have the right to attend all meetings.

The logic behind this is quite simple. Going back to the Egyptian pyramid builders and European stonemasons, one cannot expect an Apprentice in the craft to possess the same skill level of a Journeyman or Master Mason. One has to first demonstrate the knowledge and proficiency necessary to be included in the higher grades.

Master Masons, regardless of the appendant degree they have been raised to, are all regarded as equals—with one exception. The *Worshipful Master*, who is charged with governing the lodge, and *Past Grand Masters* are regarded with a level of respect commensurate with their level and service. However, since Worshipful Masters and Grand Masters have a limited term and will surrender their chair to another third degree Master Mason, even a third degree Master Mason is regarded as an equal ultimately.

Within the different rights, the appendant degrees are further grouped. For instance, in the Scottish Rite, which builds upon the ethical teachings and philosophy offered in the craft, the first set of degrees (4th to 14th) fall within "The Lodge of Perfection" and are known as the "Ineffable Degrees." The word ineffable comes from the Latin word *ineffibilis,* which translates to unspeakable, or unutterable.

Each appendant degree has its respective name: Master Traveler, Perfect Master, Master of the Brazen Serpent, Master Elect of the Temple, and Grand Master Architect, for example. They represent knowledge in various areas. The fourth appendant degree (Master Traveler) emphasizes secrecy, silence, and fidelity, while the sixth (Master of the Brazen Serpent) emphasizes faithfulness and zealousness, and teaches that devotion to one's friends and zealousness in performing one's duties are rewarding virtues.

The second set of degrees (15th and 16th) are considered the "Historical Degrees" and fall under the group called Council of Princes of Jerusalem. The teachings offered utilize settings based on the rebuilding of Jerusalem by Zerubbabel and follow the release of the Israelites from Babylon.

According to the biblical narrative, Zerubbabel was a governor of the Persian province of Judah. He is credited with leading the first group of Jews from captivity in Babylon between 538 and 520 BC. It is believed that Zerubbabel also laid the foundation of the second temple in Jerusalem soon thereafter.[27]

Since the Scottish Rite is governed by a separate central authority (Supreme Council) depending on jurisdiction, the specific names given to the 15th degree differs accordingly.

In the Southern Jurisdiction, which governs 35 states within the United States of America, the 15th degree is referred to as Knight of the East, Knight of the Sword, or Knight of the Eagle. In the Northern Jurisdiction, which oversees the bodies in fifteen states (Connecticut,

---

[27] "Zerubbabel." Wikipedia. Wikimedia Foundation. https://en.wikipedia.org/wiki/Zerubbabel.

Delaware, Illinois, Indiana, Maine, Massachusetts, Michigan, New Jersey, New Hampshire, New York, Ohio, Pennsylvania, Rhode Island, Wisconsin, and Vermont), the 15th degree is referred to as Knight of the East or Knight of the Sword (similar to Canada, England, and Whales). The 16th degree is universally known as Prince of Jerusalem.

It is a major accomplishment to obtain the highest level of degrees in either rite. Less than 10 percent of all Master Masons have obtained the 33rd degree within the Scottish Rite or the 32nd degree in the York Rite.

Key Dates Pertaining to the Emergence and Spread of Freemasonry in Europe and America

Date:	Event:
1162 - 1188	Kilwinning Abbey was established. (*) Lodge Mother Kilwinning purported to have been established. (**)
1598	William Schaw drafted a document known as the *Schaw Statutes* listing a code of rules by which the activities of operative masons in Scotland would be governed.
1599	William Schaw drafted a second set of statutes that addressed the local organization of lodges and gave the Lodge of Kilwinning (No. 0) supervisory powers over the lodges of West Scotland.
1717	Premier Grand Lodge of England was formed. Grand Master(s): Anthony Sayer (1717) George Payne (1718) John Theophilus Desaguliers (1719) The Duke of Sussex (1813)
1720	George Payne drafted *The General Regulations of a Free Mason*.
1723	The Duke of Wharton (Former Grand Master) formed anti-Masonic group called the Ancient Noble Order of the Gormogons. James Anderson's *The Constitutions of the Free-Masons* was published.

1725	Grand Lodge of Ireland was founded.
1728	Grand Lodge of France was founded. (***)
1732	Freemasonry was brought to Russia by foreign officers in the Russian service.
1734	Benjamin Franklin reprinted *The Constitutions of the Free-Masons* in Philadelphia. Benjamin Franklin was elected Grand Master in Pennsylvania.
1736	*The Constitutions of the Free-Masons* was translated into Dutch.
1736	The Grand Lodge of Scotland was founded.
1741	*The Constitutions of the Free-Masons* was translated into German.
1744	The Three Globes Lodge was founded in Berlin.
1745	*The Constitutions of the Free-Masons* was translated into French.
1772	The Three Globes became The Grand National Mother Lodge.
1773	Grand Orient de France was founded.
1782	Ivan Schwarz represented Russia at the Masonic Congress in Wilhelmsbad. Russia was recognized as the 8th Province of the Rite of Strict Observance.
1805	Grand Orient of Italy was established. (The first lodge in Italy was the English lodge *La Loggia degli Inglesi* founded in Florence in 1731.)

(*) The exact date when Kilwinning Abbey was established is unknown. Its founding is believed to have been sometime between 1162 and 1188.

(**) Lodge Mother Kilwinning is reputed to be the oldest lodge in the world. Its origin is said to have been during the 12th century when Kilwinning Abbey was established. It is believed that Kilwinning Abbey was built by stonemasons who had travelled from Europe and established a lodge there.

(***) There is debate regarding the establishment of the first Grand Lodge in France. Freemasonry itself appears to have been established in France by exiled Jacobites. The Grand Lodge of France dates its foundation to 1728. Some Grand Orient seals date the first Grand Lodge to 1736 (the split between the Grand Lodge and the Grand Orient occurred in 1773).

x. *Prince Augustus Frederick, Duke of Sussex (1773-1843)*

CHAPTER 4

Freemasonry Proliferates in Europe and America

The term "freemason" first appeared during the 17th century in the building records of Wadham College, Oxford University. Founded in 1610 by Nicholas and Dorothy Wadham, the college's building records use the terms freemason and freestone mason interchangeably. Freestone was the name given to the sandstone and limestone used for ornamental masonry. The word free also implied that the mason was not enslaved or feudally bound and could travel freely.

As legend states, a group of freemasons who had traveled from Europe to Scotland were responsible for the construction of Kilwinning Abbey (circa 1162). It is said that the same group of freemasons also established the Lodge Mother Kilwinning (No.0). Commonly referred to as the Mother Lodge of Scotland, it is reputed to be the oldest Freemason's lodge not only in Scotland, but in the world.[28]

---

[28] "Kilwinning Abbey." Wikipedia. Wikimedia Foundation. https://en.wikipedia.org/wiki/Kilwinning_Abbey.

xi. Mother Lodge building in Kilwinning, North Ayrshire, Scotland

William Schaw, who served as the Master of Works and General Warden of Master Stonemasons for James VI of Scotland, was an important figure in the development of Freemasonry in Scotland. In his capacity as Master of Works, he issued *The Statutis and ordinananceis to be obseruit by all the maister maoissounis within this realme* (also known as the *First Schaw Statutes*) on December 28, 1598. These statutes provided a set of rules for governing the activities of operative masons in Scotland. They stipulated how a lodge was to be run, how work was to be supervised, and what fines were to be levied for non-attendance of lodge meetings.

Exactly one year later, Schaw issued a second set of statutes that addressed practical matters such as health and safety concerns while working at heights. He also laid down the basic rules for proper record keeping at the lodges and predetermined specific fees.[29]

The precise reasons and mechanisms for the transition of masonic lodges from operative communities to speculative (gentlemen) fellowships are uncertain. In accordance with the *Schaw Statutes* directing all lodges in Scotland to record all important transactions, the first recorded admission of non-operative Masons was on July 3, 1634, when Sir Anthony Alexander, his elder brother, Lord Alexander, and Sir Alexander Strachan of Thornton were initiated into the Lodge of Edinburgh. It is uncertain as to when speculative or non-operative Masons first appeared in England, as no written records were kept until 1723. By October of 1646, the emergence of

---

[29] "William Shaw." Wikipedia. Wikimedia Foundation. https://en.wikipedia.org/wiki/William_Schaw.

mixed lodges consisting of both operative and speculative Masons were on the rise in Scotland.

On June 24, 1717, the Premier Grand Lodge of England was formed. The new grand lodge introduced many changes that substantially deviated from the ancient practices of the craft and pursued a policy of self-promotion and expansion, sweeping throughout England, Wales, and abroad. This did not sit well with the other Freemasons. As a result, these men formed their own lodges or joined unaffiliated lodges in London.[30]

In 1751, six of these lodges joined together to form a rival grand lodge, which became an umbrella organization for all the other unaffiliated lodges in England. They called themselves the Grand Lodge of the Most Ancient and Honourable Fraternity of Free and Accepted Masons, more commonly referred to as the Ancient Grand Lodge of England. Hence, the Premier Grand Lodge of England came to be known as the *Moderns*, and the Ancient Grand Lodge of England was recognized as the *Ancients*. The grand lodges of Ireland and Scotland viewed the innovations of the Moderns with suspicion, which enabled the Ancients to flourish.[31]

Gradually, the two lodges moved toward a union which was accelerated by the Napoleonic Wars. The leaders of the Ancients, the Moderns, and the Grand Lodge of Scotland thought it was prudent to

---

[30] "Premier Grand Lodge of England." Wikipedia. Wikimedia Foundation. https://en.wikipedia.org/wiki/Premier_Grand_Lodge_of_England.
[31] "Antient Grand Lodge of England." Wikipedia. Wikimedia Foundation. https://en.wikipedia.org/wiki/Antient_Grand_Lodge_of_England.

work together during this time to prevent the prohibition of their respective organizations. A union was achieved on December 27, 1813, when The Premier Grand Lodge of England merged with the Ancient Grand Lodge of England to form the United Grand Lodge of England (UGLE). UGLE became the governing body for the majority of Freemasons within England and Wales with lodges in other, predominantly former British Empire and Commonwealth countries outside the United Kingdom.[32]

As Freemasonry took its foothold in Scotland, England, Wales, and Ireland, it also proliferated Europe.

France

Although there is some disagreement as to when the first grand lodge was founded in France, it appears that Freemasonry itself was established in France by the exiled Jacobites from England. Jacobitism was a political movement in England and Ireland which sought to restore the deposed Roman Catholic King James II to the throne.

The Grand Orient de France (GODF) is the largest of several Masonic organizations in France and the oldest in continental Europe. The GODF was founded in 1773 from the remnants of the older Grand Lodge of France. The Grand Orient is generally considered to be the mother lodge of traditional Liberal, or Continental Freemasonry.

---

[32] "United Grand Lodge of England." Wikipedia. Wikimedia Foundation. https://en.wikipedia.org/wiki/United_Grand_Lodge_of_England.

Continental Freemasonry resulted from a rift within Freemasonry which grew from the GODF's alteration of its constitution in 1877. The GODF adopted a more liberal approach to admitting candidates by not requiring that they declare a belief in a supreme being. Consequently, the GODF admitted atheists while lodges operating in the Anglo-American tradition did not.[33]

Italy

The first lodge in Italy was an English lodge established in 1731 and known as La Loggia degli Inglesi. Freemasonry spread quickly in Italy despite the Papal bans, and in 1805 the Grand Orient of Italy was founded.[34]

Germany

The first German Grand Lodge was founded in Berlin in 1744. The Three Globes, as it was known, was based on the English model and went on to become the Grand National Mother Lodge (Große National-Mutterloge, Zu den drei Weltkugeln) in 1772. It was the oldest among eight recognized Masonic grand lodges which existed in Germany until their abolition in 1935 by the German Reich.[35]

---

[33] "Grand Orient De France." Wikipedia. Wikimedia Foundation. https://en.wikipedia.org/wiki/Grand_Orient_De_France.
[34] "Grand Orient of Italy." Wikipedia. Wikimedia Foundation. https://en.wikipedia.org/wiki/Grand_Orient_of_Italy.
[35] "Grand National Mother Lodge, "The Three Globes"." Wikipedia. Wikimedia Foundation. https://en.wikipedia.org/wiki/Grand_National_Mother_Lodge,%22The_Three_Globes%22.

xii. GODF - The Grand Temple, the largest conference and meeting room where several lodges occasionally meet

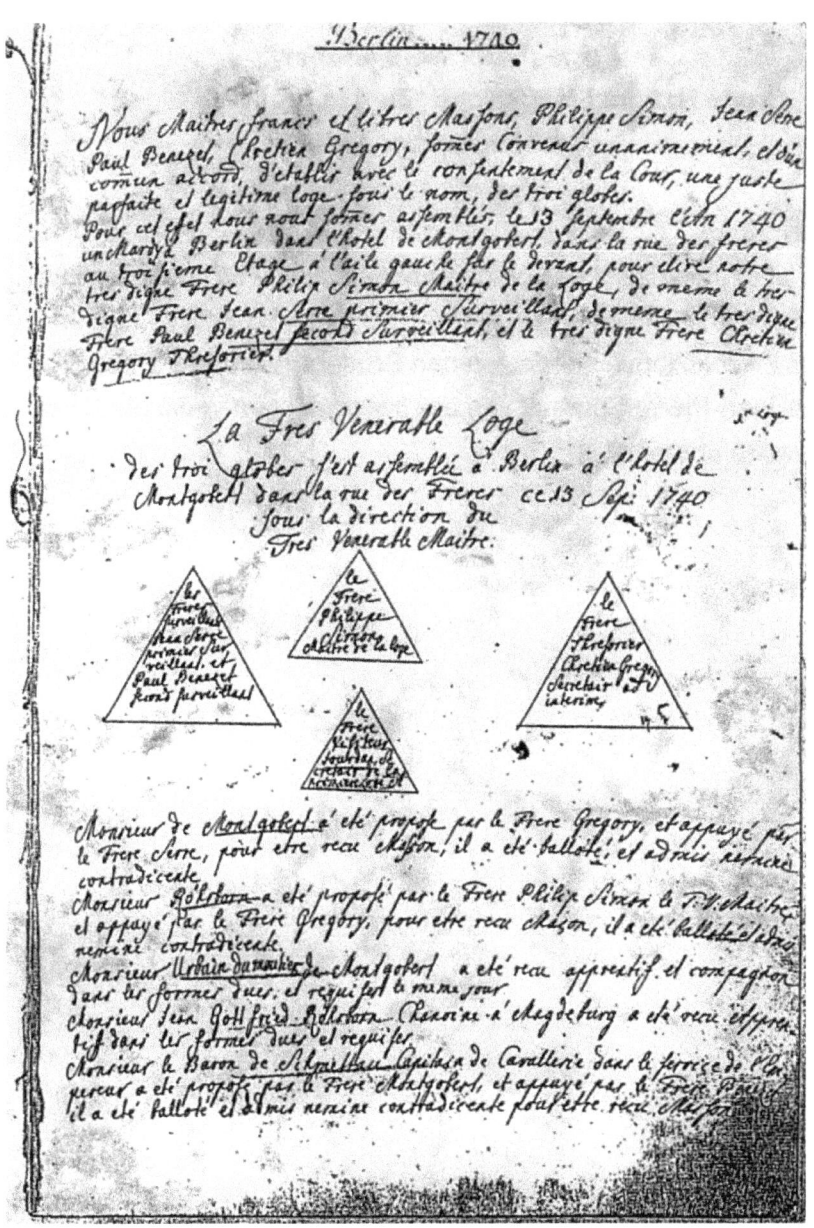

xiii. Minutes from the founding of Große National-Mutterloge, Zu den drei Weltkugeln

Russia

Freemasonry reached Russia in the early 1700s via foreign officers serving in the Russian military. Records indicate that James Keith was a Master of a lodge in Saint Petersburg from 1732 to 1734. Several years later his cousin, John Keith, the 3rd Earl of Kintore was appointed Provincial Grand Master of Russia by the Grand Lodge of England.

Ivan Perfilievich Yelagin (1725–94), a Russian historian who acted as unofficial secretary to Catherine the Great in the early years of her reign, is credited with reorganizing Russian Freemasonry, which united over 14 lodges and approximately 400 government officials. He later managed to secure the authorization for establishing the first Russian Grand Lodge through the English Grand Lodge and became its Provincial Grand Master.[36]

North America

From the British Isles, Freemasonry spread to North America during the Colonial period. All the original English Grand Lodges issued charters to individual lodges in America, but the Ancients and the Moderns were the most prolific.

There were a significant number of lodges that were attached to British Army regiments. A group of African Americans who had been rejected by the Boston lodges were initiated into Lodge No. 441 chartered by

---

[36] "History of Freemasonry in Russia." Wikipedia. Wikimedia Foundation. https://en.wikipedia.org/wiki/History_of_Freemasonry_in_Russia.

xiv. Ivan Perfilievich Yelagin (1725–94)

the Grand Lodge of Ireland. This lodge was attached to the 38th (1st Staffordshire) Regiment of Foot, an infantry regiment of the British Army. When the regiment left, they left behind a permit allowing the fifteen African American men to form the African Lodge No. 1. Later, their Master, Prince Hall, applied for a charter with the Moderns, which was granted on September 29, 1784. The African Lodge No. 1 evolved into the African Lodge No. 459, and later became a provincial grand lodge with Prince Hall as its Provincial Grand Master. Following Hall's death in 1807, the provincial lodges reconstituted themselves as the African Grand Lodge and later became the Prince Hall Grand Lodge in 1847.[37]

Mexico

Freemasonry arrived in colonial Mexico during the second half of the 18th century, brought by French immigrants who settled in the capital. The first Masonic lodge of Mexico, Arquitectura Moral, was founded in 1806. The first Grand Lodge of Mexico, Scottish Rite, was created in 1813.

Beginning with the Mexican War of Independence in 1821 until 1982, many of Mexico's leaders were said to have been Freemasons.[38]

---

[37] "History of Freemasonry." Masonic Service Association of North America. http://www.msana.com/historyfm.asp.
[38] "Freemasonry in Mexico." Wikipedia. Wikimedia Foundation. https://en.wikipedia.org/wiki/Freemasonry_in_Mexico.

xv. Portrait of Prince Hall (c.1735 – December 4, 1807)

The Gormogons

It bears mentioning that as Freemasonry began to gain a strong foothold around the world, anti-Masonic organizations also surfaced from time to time, attempting to discredit the brotherhood. One such organization was the Ancient Noble Order of the Gormogons, established in 1723 by former Freemason, Philip Wharton, the First Duke of Wharton.

Philip Wharton was a powerful Jacobite politician, who became Grand Master of the Premier Grand Lodge of England in 1722. However, his lifestyle was not endorsed by the other Freemasons, and soon his position as Grand Master was challenged. In order to maintain unity among the fraternity, Wharton was allowed to remain Grand Master until the following year, after which time the Earl of Dalkeith became the new elected Grand Master. Angered by the election, Wharton challenged Dalkeith's appointment, but it was upheld by the Grand Lodge. It is not clear if Wharton unofficially walked out or was expelled, but he went on to form the short-lived Ancient Noble Order of the Gormogons afterwards. Few written records have survived over the years attesting to the true goal and purpose of the Gormogons, but it can be established from the various articles the group had published that they existed merely to mock Freemasonry.[39]

---

[39] "Gormogons." Wikipedia. Wikimedia Foundation. https://en.wikipedia.org/wiki/Gormogons

Key Dates in Chinese History

Date:	Event:
1644	The Qing dynasty began. Founded by the Manchus, it was the last imperial dynasty in China. The Manchus utilized the Confucian norms of traditional Chinese government during their rule.
1759	Freemasons arrived in China aboard the Prins Carl, a merchant ship belonging to the Swedish East India Company. The ship docked at a port in Canton (Guangzhou).
1767	Amity Lodge No. 407 was established in Canton (Guangzhou) under the jurisdiction of the Grand Lodge of England. Regular meetings were held for 46 years, but the lodge ceased operating in 1813 when it's charter was not renewed when the two Grand English Lodges united in London.
1795	Freemason, Isaac Titsingh, traveled to China representing both the Dutch and the Dutch East India Company (VOC) interests at the court of Qing Emperor Qianlong.
1839	The First Opium War began.
1842	The Treaty of Nanking was signed ceding the island of Hong Kong to the British. Five treaty ports were established (Shanghai, Canton (Guangzhou), Ningpo, Fuchow, and Amoy).
1844	The Royal Sussex Lodge was established in Hong Kong.
1846	The Zetland Lodge was established in Hong Kong.

1849	The first Masonic meetings were held in Shanghai.
1850	The Taiping Rebellion, fought between the Qing dynasty and the Christian millenarian movement of the Taiping Heavenly Kingdom, began.
1856	The Second Opium War began.
1860	Qing troops supported by European officers under the command of Frederick Townsend Ward assisted by local strategic support of the French diplomat Albert-Édouard Levieux de Caligny (the Ever Victorious Army) defeated the Taiping rebels in Shanghai. A second set of treaty ports were established (Nanjing, Beijing, Harbin, and Chengdu) involving numerous foreign powers. All foreign traders gained rights to travel within China.
1864	The Qing forces regained control of Nanjing and ended the Taiping Rebellion.
1889	A lieutenant in the Imperial Chinese Navy became the first known Chinese person to become a Freemason. He was initiated at the Lodge Star of Southern China No. 2013 EC in Canton (Guangzhou).
1894	First Sino-Japanese War began.
1895	The Treaty of Shimonoseki was signed ceding Taiwan to Japan.
1898	The Northern Star of China Lodge was established in Yingkou (Newchwang).

1899	The Boxer Rebellion began. It was spurred on by proto-nationalist sentiments and opposition to Western colonialism and the Christian missionary activity that was associated with it.
1903	The Kiukiang Lodge No. 2984 was established followed by lodges in Qingdao, Wei Hai Wei, and Tienjin.
1908	Empress Dowager Cixi passed away.
1911	The Wuchang Uprising against the Qing dynasty began. The Xinhai Revolution overthrew the Qing dynasty and established the Republic of China (ROC).

CHAPTER 5

Confucianism, Taoism, and Freemasonry

Throughout history, there are many things which have left their indelible fingerprints upon a civilization. Sometimes these influences originate from within a culture and other times they infiltrate society from the outside.

Without question, Confucianism and Taoism are two of the most influential philosophies/ religious beliefs that have coexisted in China, having been part of the culture for well over 2,500 years. They have both had an amazing impact on the growth, traditions, religions, and beliefs of the Chinese people and have attracted countless followers.

Although both Confucianism and Taoism share common beliefs about man, society, and the universe, there are notable key differences within their teachings. Confucianism focuses on the relationship between man and society whereas, Taoism emphasizes the relationship between man and nature.

Confucianism encourages social harmony and mutual respect between people and between governments. It further stipulates that knowledge and education are vital in understanding the moral and ethical principles required for a proper society.

Confucianism was created by a politician, musician, and philosopher named Confucius. Born in 551 BC, Confucius traveled extensively throughout China, first as a government employee and later as a political advisor to the rulers of the Chou dynasty (1122–221 BC). In later life, Confucius abandoned politics in favor of teaching a small group of students. Following his death in 479 BC, the ethical and moral teachings of Confucius were written down by his students and became known as the *Lúnyǔ*, or *Analects of Confucius*.

The goal of Confucianism is simple. Each person is required to act with virtue in all social matters: family, community, state, and kingdom, to ensure order and unity. Hence, Confucianism became the social philosophy of China from 202 BC until the end of dynastic rule in 1911.[40]

The objective of Taoism is more esoteric. It calls for a person to align harmoniously with the "Tao" and achieve immortality by taking the right path in life. It focuses on the human experience, the feeling of oneness with the universe. The Tao, although not easily understood, can be defined in its simplest form as the natural order of the universe.

---

[40] "Taoism and Confucianism - Ancient Philosophies." Ushistory.org. Independence Hall Association. https://www.ushistory.org/civ/9e.asp.

xvi. Confucius (Portrait by Qiu Ying (1494–1552)

xvii. Laozi

Laozi, the Chinese philosopher credited as the founder of philosophical Taoism is believed to have authored *Tao Te Ching*, a work which has influenced millions during the last 2,500 years. Very little is known about his life; he may or may not have actually existed. What we do know is that although Laozi is credited with founding philosophical Taoism, Taoism itself predates Laozi as he refers to "The Tao masters of antiquity" in *Tao Te Ching*.[41]

According to Taoism, the entire universe and everything in it flows with a mysterious, unknown force called the Tao. Translated literally as the way, Tao has many different meanings. It is the name that describes ultimate reality and explains the powers that drive the universe and the wonder of human nature. Taoists believe that everything is one. For instance, there would be no love without hate.

Over time, a divergent Taoist religion emerged. While religious Taoism shared some of the same beliefs of philosophical Taoism, it also called for the worship of various gods and ancestors, a practice that began during the Shang dynasty (1600 to 1046 BC). Other religious elements included the cultivation of bodily energy called *chi*, the creation of a system of morals, and use of alchemy in an attempt to attain immortality. Taoist philosophy and religion eventually found their way into all Asian cultures influenced by China, particularly those of Vietnam, Japan, and Korea.

---

[41] "Taoism and Confucianism - Ancient Philosophies." Ushistory.org.

Taoism was the dominant religion of the Han dynasty. Buddhism also flourished in China during the Han dynasty following its arrival at approximately the 1st century AD. It is believed that Buddhism reached China from North India through the Silk Road. Confucianism, on the other hand, was more of a philosophy rather than a religion at the time. It was during the Han dynasty that China first truly embraced Confucianism. Despite it not being a religion, it became one of the most important ideological beliefs during that era.

The Han dynasty also expanded the lucrative silk trade via the Silk Road. The Silk Road commonly refers to the ancient network of trade routes connecting the East and the West. The Han dynasty extended the Central Asian section of the trade routes around 114 BC aided by the missions and explorations of the Chinese imperial envoy Zhang Qian.[42]

Freemasonry Reaches China

Though silk was the major trade item, the Silk Road also served as a route for cultural trade among the civilizations along its network.

This cultural trade was responsible for Freemasonry gaining a foothold in Chinese society. The craft spread like wildfire throughout Europe during the 18th century. From that point, armed forces personnel and merchants who were Freemasons brought Freemasonry to the United States, India, and the East.

---

[42] "Silk Road." Encyclopædia Britannica. Encyclopædia Britannica, Inc. https://www.britannica.com/topic/Silk-Road-trade-route.

Freemasonry reached China on July 8, 1759. The Prins Carl, a merchant ship belonging to the Swedish East India Company, docked at a port in Canton (Guangzhou) with Captain Baltzar Grubb in charge.[43] The men on board were Freemasons who carried with them a document which gave them permission to gather and hold meetings wherever they came ashore. According to Masonic records, the first meeting was held in late 1759.

The Swedish East India Company (SOIC) was founded in Gothenburg, Sweden in 1731 following the successes of the Dutch East India Company and the British East India Company.[44]

The Grill family were ironmasters that were based all over Europe, and they were also influential members and directors of the Swedish East India Company (SOIC). Claes Grill II (September 2, 1750 – August 2, 1816), the son of Abraham Grill II, was a Freemason and a member of the London Emulation Lodge of Improvement.

When the two rival English lodges united in 1813, the Lodge of Reconciliation was created with an equal number of chosen representatives from each of the lodges for the purpose of maintaining uniformity in the making, passing, and raising of Freemasons throughout England. The lodge was dissolved in 1816, but the Emulation Lodge of Improvement was formed to continue the work of

---

[43] Koninck, Christian. (1978) "The Maritime Routes of the Swedish East India Company During Its First and Second Charter (1731-1766)." Taylor and Frances Online. www.tandfonline.com/doi/abs/10.1080/03583322.1978.10407895
[44] "Swedish East India Company." Wikipedia. Wikimedia Foundation. https://en.wikipedia.org/wiki/Swedish_East_India_Company.

the Lodge of Reconciliation.[45]

In addition to the Grill family, other Freemasons served as directors of the Swedish East India Company and greatly influenced the events which unfolded in China. William Chalmers, a Swedish merchant and Freemason, became a director of the Swedish East India Company in 1783. He was appointed as their resident representative in Canton where he remained for ten years before returning home.[46]

Canton had historically been the major southern port in China and the main outlet for the country's tea, rhubarb, silk, spices, and handcrafted articles that were sought by Western traders. Consequently, the British East India Company, which had a monopoly on British trade with China, made Canton its major Chinese port early in the 17th century, and other Western trading companies soon followed their example.

With the competition intensifying, the British pushed to expand trade to the ports in northern China. Predictably, the government responded by tightening their regulations on foreign traders. In 1757, the Qing Emperor issued a decree explicitly making Canton the only port open to foreign commerce. Foreign merchants became subject to numerous challenging regulations including the exclusion of foreign warships from the area, the prohibition of foreign women and firearms, and a

---

[45] Cozens, Ken. "Swedes, Merchants, Freemasons and East India Company Agents in 18th Century East London." Port Towns and Urban Cultures. https://porttowns.port.ac.uk/swedes-merchants/.
[46] "William Chalmers (merchant)." Wikipedia. Wikimedia Foundation. https://en.wikipedia.ord/wiki/William_Chalmers_(merchant).

xviii. William Chalmers, Director of the Swedish East India Company and a Freemason

variety of restrictions on the merchants' personal freedom.[47]

In the early 19th century, the Qing dynasty was at the height of its power. British traders began to get irritated by the restrictions imposed upon them by the Qing Emperor, and the complaints grew more

---

[47] "Canton System." Encyclopædia Britannica. Encyclopædia Britannica, Inc. https://www.britannica.com/event/Canton-system.

numerous with the abolition of the East India Company monopoly in 1834, resulting in the influx of private traders into China. At the same time, the British trade increasingly centered on the illegal importation of opium from India to China as a means of paying for the British purchases of tea and silk. Chinese attempts to halt the opium trade, which had caused social and economic disruption, resulted in the First Opium War (1839–42) between Britain and China. The British were victorious, and the Qing government was forced to sign the Treaty of Nanking. This unequal treaty created five treaty ports (Chinese ports open to trade with foreigners) in which foreigners could live and work outside Chinese legal jurisdiction, trading with whomever they pleased. It also resulted in the cession of Hong Kong to the British. (China regained control of Hong Kong in 1997.)

However, the Anglo-Chinese disputes over trade did not end there. The Second Opium War erupted in 1856 and lasted through 1860. In June of 1858, the first part of the war ended with the four Treaties of Tientsin, to which Britain, France, Russia, and the United States were parties. These treaties, which the Chinese initially refused to ratify, opened 11 more ports to Western trade.[48]

As the Western powers were busy carving up China, the Qing ministers prevailed upon the Xianfeng Emperor in June of 1858 to resist the Western encroachment. Hence, the second phase of the war ensued.

Anglo-French forces entered Beijing on October 6, 1858. The Qing

---

[48] "Opium Wars." Encyclopædia Britannica. Encyclopædia Britannica, Inc. https://www.britannica.com/topic/Opium-Wars.

army was devastated at this point and the Xianfeng Emperor fled the capital leaving his brother, Prince Gong, to take charge of the peace negotiations. Prince Gong ratified the Treaty of Tianjin during the Convention of Beijing on October 18, 1860, finally bringing the Second Opium War to an end.

Soon after the British acquired Hong Kong, they established two Masonic lodges: the Royal Sussex Lodge in 1844 and the Zetland Lodge in 1846. The Sussex Lodge was moved to Guangzhou and then to Shanghai, but it was reestablished in Hong Kong in 1952. The Zetland Lodge had remained in Hong Kong since its formation, but its original building was destroyed when the Japanese invaded Hong Kong. A second Masonic hall was erected on the site of an old hotel and dedicated in 1950.

The first Masonic meetings were held in Shanghai in 1849 in various private homes. From that point, lodges surfaced in Kiukiang, Qingdao, Wei Hai Wei, and Tienjin. Eventually, lodges spread to the treaty ports and to inland cities such as Nanjing, Beijing, Harbin, and Chengdu. These lodges operated under charters granted by England, America, Scotland, Ireland, Germany, and later the Philippines.

The Chinese Freemasons

During the Qing dynasty the government imposed restrictions on Chinese people and it was almost impossible for a Chinese to become a Freemason. The first known Chinese to become a Freemason was a lieutenant in the Imperial Chinese Navy stationed in Guangzhou in 1889. However, it is believed that a secret society which was a predecessor to the modern Chinese Freemasons had existed approximately one hundred years earlier, a fact further corroborated by the Grand Lodge of British Columbia.

This secret society was known as the *Hongmen*. The Hongmen was just one of the names used for the largest secret society known as the *Tiandihui*. The Tiandihui utilized a number of aliases, such as the Hongmen, to deceive the Qing dynasty as they propagated to various places.

The Tiandihui literally translates to the Society of the Heaven and the Earth. This society played a crucial role during many of the pivotal junctures in Chinese history as it spread throughout the different counties and provinces.

According to the First Historical Archives in Beijing, the Tiandihui was established in 1762 by Li Amin, Zhu Dingyuan, Tao Yuan, and a monk known as Ti Xi. The 18th century saw a significant increase of such societies, some of which were devoted to overthrowing the Qing government. They had adopted a slogan, "Fang Ching Fu Ming (Oppose Qing and restore Ming)."[49] This view was further perpetuated by a Freemason named Sun Yat-sen and other revolutionaries.

---

[49] "Tiandihui." Wikipedia. Wikimedia Foundation. https://en.wikipedia.org/wiki/Tiandihui.

xix. Prince Gong

However, in her book entitled, *The Origins of the Tiandihui*, Dian Murray attempts to dispel this perception. She claims that according to the Qing dynasty archives, the Tiandihui was founded not as a political movement but as a mutual aid brotherhood in 1761.[50]

Sun Yat-sen

Sun Yat-sen, a Chinese physician, revolutionary and Freemason, was also the first provisional president and founding father of the Republic of China. He played an instrumental role in the overthrow of the Qing dynasty during the years leading up to the Xinhai Revolution. Sun also co-founded the Kuomintang (Nationalist Party of China), serving as its first leader.

Sun joined the Chinese Freemasons on January 10, 1904. He served as the Hong Gun, the highest position that one could hold within the lodge, similar to the Western Freemasons' Grand Master, and used this group to leverage his overseas travels to garner further financial and resource support for his revolution.

Sun Yat-sen was the son of poor farmers residing in the small village of Cuiheng, in China's Xiangshan County. He traveled to Honolulu in 1879 to live with his brother, Sun Mei, who had emigrated to Hawaii in 1871 as a laborer. It was there where he received his Western education, his Christian faith, and the funds to lead a revolution. He was troubled by the way China, which had clung to its traditional ways under the conservative Qing dynasty, suffered humiliation at the hands

---

[50] Murray, Dian H. and Baoqi, Qin. The Origins of the Tiandihui: The Chinese Triads in Legend and History. Stanford University Press. July 1, 1994.

of the more technologically advanced nations. He knew that the only way to usher in change and modernization was by overthrowing the Qing dynasty.

Having been educated as a physician, he quit his medical practice in 1894 in order to devote his time to transforming China. He founded an organization called the Xingzhonghui (the Revive China Society), which became the forerunner to the Tongmenghui. The Tongmenghui was a secret society and underground resistance movement founded in Tokyo in August of 1905. This group eventually evolved into the Kuomintang (the Nationalist Party of China).

The Xingzhonghui came into existence in Honolulu on November 24, 1894, as Sun was in exile from China at the time. Its members swore an oath to "expel Tatar barbarians, revive Zhonghua, and establish a unified government."[51] The Tatars, of course, were the Manchu who had established the Qing dynasty. The Zhonghua were the ancestors of the Han ethnic group in China. The perception was that they represented the civilized society which stood distinct and in contrast to the barbaric peoples (The Manchu).

In 1895, China suffered a serious defeat during the First Sino-Japanese War. As a result, two schools of thought emerged. One group of intellectuals, which included Kang Youwei and Liang Qichao, contended that the Qing government could restore its legitimacy by successfully modernizing China. They felt that overthrowing the Qing

---

[51] "Sun Yat-Sen." Wikipedia. Wikimedia Foundation. https://en.wikipedia.org/wiki/Sun_Yat-sen.

xx. Dr. Sun Yat-sen pictured (seated, second from right) with the Chicago branch of the Tongmenghui in 1911.

xxi. Dr. Sun Yat-sen (seated) and Chiang Kai-shek

would result in chaos and would lead to China being further carved up by the imperialists. A second group, which consisted of Sun Yat-sen and Zou Rong among others, wanted a revolution to replace the dynastic system with a modern nation-state in the form of a republic.

Sun Yat-sen returned to Hong Kong in early 1895, and met with Yeung Ku-wan, the leader of the Furen Literary Society. Yeung too had received a western education at St. Paul's College in Hong Kong, one of the world's earliest Anglo-Chinese schools.

The Furen Literary Society, also known as the Chinese Patriotic Mutual Improvement Association, was founded in Hong Kong in 1892 with the purpose of advocating the overthrow of the Qing government and establishing a republic in China.

Following their meeting in 1895, Sun Yat-sen and Yeung Ku-wan were eager to take advantage of the uneasy political situation created by the First Sino-Japanese War. They decided to merge the Furen Literary Society with the Revive China Society to form the Hong Kong chapter of the later and set up a mock business called the Kuen Hang Club to disguise their revolutionary activities. In October of 1895 the Society planned to launch an uprising in Guangzhou. Unfortunately, their plans were leaked and more than 70 members of the organization were captured by the Qing government. Under pressure from the Qing government, the British colonial authorities banned Yeung and Sun from Hong Kong for the next five years.

Yeung travelled to Johannesburg via Singapore and later arrived in Japan. He remained in Japan from 1896 to 1899 where he worked to expand the Revive China Society and spread its doctrines.[52]

Sun spent 16 years in exile in Europe, the United States, Canada, and Japan, raising money for his revolutionary work and to support uprisings in China. He traveled to Japan by way of Canada. Arriving in August of 1897 he was met by Miyazaki Torazo, better known by his pen name, Miyazaki Toten.[53]

Miyazaki was a Japanese philosopher and revolutionary activist. Born in Kumamoto, he was the younger brother of Tamizo and Hachiro, both social activists in their own right. Miyazaki's family had experienced difficult times due to the rural impact of the Meiji government's attempts to monetize the tax system. All three brothers pushed for reform with the belief that effecting reform in China would be the best way to inspire changes within Japan. Miyazaki converted to Christianity in 1887 only to abandon his faith two years later. He was an ardent supporter of Sun Yat-sen and devoted his entire life to ensuring his friend's success.[54]

Miyazaki introduced Sun to many influential Japanese, including the elder statesmen Okuma Shigenobu, Soejima Taneomi, and Inukai

---

[52] "Furen Literary Society." Wikipedia. Wikimedia Foundation.
https://en.wikipedia.org/wiki/Furen_Literary_Society.
[53] "Sun Yat-Sen." Wikipedia.
[54] "Toten Miyazaki." Wikipedia. Wikimedia Foundation.
https://en.wikipedia.org/wiki/T%C5%8Dten_Miyazaki.

Tsuyoshi, from whom Sun was to receive both political and financial assistance.

Okuma Shigenobu was a Japanese politician who served as Japan's Prime Minister from April 16, 1914 to October 9, 1916. He was an early advocate of Western science and culture, as well as a Masonic sympathizer. It is purported that he was the foreign minister who entered into a gentleman's agreement with the Masonic bodies in Japan to allow them to hold meetings without police supervision. Japanese law stated that police approval was required for all public meetings, both indoors and outdoors. Initially, this law did not affect the foreign Masons as Japanese law did not apply to foreigners. However, that changed in 1894 when the United Kingdom and Japan signed the Treaty of Commerce and Navigation which, among other things, granted the citizens of each country full access, and thus full accountability, to the legal system of the other nation.

Sun traveled to Singapore on September 7, 1900, on a mission to rescue his friend and supporter, Miyazaki Toten, who had been arrested there. This action resulted in his own arrest and his banishment from Singapore for a period of five years.

On October 22, 1900, after having secured the political and financial assistance necessary, Sun launched the Huizhou uprising in Guangdong. Like the previous uprisings this too ended in failure.

However, the year 1903 marked a significant turning point for Sun's movement. He received increasing support from the educated class, the most prestigious and influential group in China. In 1904, he established several revolutionary cells in Europe, and in 1905 he became head of a revolutionary coalition known as the Chinese United League or the Chinese Revolutionary Alliance (Tongmenghui), in Tokyo.

The group came into existence on August 20, 1905 and was comprised of various dissident Chinese groups who had either fled to Japan or had gone there to study. Sun openly advocated military activism to overthrow the Qing government, and the movement was generously supported by overseas Chinese funds, with the bulk of the funding coming from the Tiandihui, the claimed predecessors to the modern Chinese Freemasons.[55]

Situ Meitang

Sun joined the Chinese Freemasons, known as the *Chee Kong Tong* overseas, while he was in Hawaii in 1904. He had been living in San Francisco with a man named Situ Meitang. Situ who had devoted nearly his entire life to aiding the Chinese living overseas eventually served as the leader of the China Zhi Gong Party in the Americas.

The China Zhi Gong Party or the China Party for Public Interest is one of the eight legally recognized political parties in the People's Republic of China today. The organization was founded on October 10, 1925 and originated from the overseas Hung Society or Hongmen (Chinese Freemasons) based in San Francisco.

---

[55] "Sun Yat-Sen." Wikipedia.

xxii. Tokyo, 1900 (from left) Suenage Takashi, Uchida Ryohei, Miyazaki Torazo, Koyama Yutaro, Kiyofuji Koshichiro, and Sun Yat-sen

The party relocated its headquarters to Hong Kong in 1926 and currently follows the direction of the Communist Party of China and is represented in the Chinese People's Political Consultative Conference. The China Zhi Gong Party is designated as the party for Chinese people who have returned from overseas, their relatives, and noted figures and scholars who have overseas ties.

At their peak, there were six Chinese Society Halls operated by the Chinese Freemasons in Maui. Their purpose was to provide services to immigrant Chinese workers who labored at the sugarcane farms.

Chinese workers, consisting largely of single men, began to arrive in Hawaii in 1852 to work on the sugarcane plantations. After their contracts expired they remained in Hawaii and took up other trades. The Chinese Masonic societies cropped up to provide religious and political assistance as well as mutual aid, friendship, and funerary benefits when these workers died.

Situ Meitang was born in Guangdong province in 1868 and came to San Francisco at the age of 12 in search of work. He went on to sponsor Sun Yat-sen's revolution, befriended Franklin D. Roosevelt before he became the President of the United States, and led the overseas Chinese communities in fundraising during the War of Resistance Against Japanese Aggression (1931-45).

xxiii. Situ Meitang

He initially held several jobs including that of a restaurant worker, a butler, and a chef in the United States Navy. He met Sun in 1904, and when the revolutionary leader could not make ends meet after the failed uprisings, Situ mortgaged four Chee Kong Tong properties in Canada to help sponsor him. He reportedly raised $150,000 to fund Sun's revolution.

When Situ moved to New York City in 1905, Franklin Roosevelt was still a young attorney and served as a legal consultant for the 37-year-old Situ Meitang. The two men formed an enduring friendship, which may have been the reason why President Roosevelt asked the United States Congress to act promptly on a pending bill to repeal the Chinese Exclusion Laws in October of 1943. Later on, their friendship may have been further cemented by the fact that both men were Freemasons. [56]

Franklin Roosevelt was initiated into the Masonic order on October 10, 1911, passed on November 14, 1911, and raised on November 28, 1911 in the Holland Lodge, No. 8, located in New York City. He petitioned the Ancient Accepted Scottish Rite in the Albany Consistory of New York on February 28, 1929, and received his 32nd degree the same day.[57]

---

[56] (Situ Meitang)维基媒体项目贡献者． "司徒美堂." 维基百科，自由的百科全, Wikimedia Foundation, Inc. https://zh-m-wikipedia-org.translate.goog/zh-hans/%E5%8F%B8%E5%BE%92%E7%BE%8E%E5%A0%82?_x_tr_sl=zh-CN&_x_tr_tl=en&_x_tr_hl=en&_x_tr_pto=sc.
[57] "Freemasons." In Roosevelt History. https://fdrlibrary.wordpress.com/tag/freemasons/.

xxiv. The China Zhi Gong Party

xxv. Franklin D. Roosevelt designated in the photograph as a 32nd degree Freemason

The End of the Qing Dynasty

Sun Yat-sen returned to Singapore in June of 1905 and urged the local Chinese merchants there to establish a Singapore chapter of the Tongmenghui. The Singapore chapter was officially established on April 6, 1906, and had 400 members. It became the regional headquarters for all branches in Southeast Asia in 1908. Sun and his followers traveled from Singapore to Malaya and Indonesia to spread their revolutionary message. By this time the Tongmenghui already had over twenty branches with more than 3,000 members worldwide.

However, as all the revolts Sun and the others organized ended in failure, his followers fell into despair; he was shunned by foreign governments and outside financial contributions declined. Even Japan, where Sun had found refuge, gave him a sum of money and asked him to leave the country in 1907.

Sun spent a year touring Europe and the United States. He returned to Asia in June of 1910, but left for the West once again in December following a meeting with other revolutionaries during which a decision was made to capture Guangzhou. Sun managed to raise more money in Canada and the United States, but the uprising of April 27 in Guangzhou (known as the March 29 Revolution because of its date in the Chinese calendar) fared no better than the earlier plots.

In the meantime, in an effort to preserve its rule, the Qing government reorganized its army, instituted a school system, abolished the civil-service examinations, reconstructed many government organizations, and convened provincial and national assemblies. Nevertheless, the educated class remained dissatisfied with the speed with which change was taking place, and the regime began to rapidly lose its hold.

In 1911 a rebellion broke out in the province of Sichuan which the government failed to suppress, leading to subsequent attacks. In October of the same year, a local revolutionary group in Wuchang (The Wuchang Uprising; October 10–December 1, 1911) instigated another rebellion and managed to overthrow the provincial government. Its success inspired several other uprisings, which quickly spread across southern China and constituted the beginning of the Xinhai Revolution. The Wuchang Uprising and the eventual revolution directly led to the downfall of the Qing dynasty.

Sun Yat-sen learned of the Wuchang Uprising from the newspapers while he was in the United States. He returned to Shanghai in December of 1911. On Feb. 12, 1912, the Qing Emperor, Puyi, abdicated.

Shortly after the Xinhai Revolution, Sun Yat-sen and Song Jiaoren founded the Nationalist Party of China or the Kuomintang of China (KMT). The predecessor of the Kuomintang was the Tongmenghui (Chinese Revolutionary Alliance), which Sun Yat-sen, Song Jiaoren, and others had founded in Tokyo on August 20, 1905.

xxvi. Puyi in 1961, flanked by Xiong Bingkun, a commander in the Wuchang Uprising, and Lu Zhonglin, who took part in Puyi's expulsion from the Forbidden City in 1924

In 1913, the party participated in the first Chinese parliament (The National Assembly of the Republic of China), which represented the first free democratic legislature in Chinese history. Sun Yat-sen the Freemason became the National Assembly's Provisional President, a position which he was later forced to turn over to Yuan Shikai. The National Assembly was disbanded on January 10, 1914 when President Yuan Shikai assumed dictatorial power and declared himself the Emperor of China.

Following the disbanding of the National Assembly in January of 1914, Sun Yat-sen took measures to reorganize it, further strengthening it. Initially, the party structure was based on the model of a Chinese secret society and later, under Soviet guidance, on that of the Bolshevik party. The Nationalist Party owed its early successes largely to Soviet aid and advice.

Although these actions bolstered the Nationalists, there was still considerable opposition to Sun's authority when he died of cancer in Beijing in March of 1925.[58]

The Post-Revolution Chinese Freemasons

During the late 19th century the Hongmen society branched out overseas, assembling in Chinese communities located in the United States, Canada, and Australia. It is estimated that there are approximately 300,000 members worldwide. While membership is predominantly ethnic Chinese, there are also a small number of Japanese and non-Asian American members.

The Hongmen members worldwide observe certain common traditions. They all stress their patriotic origin, revere Guan Yu, and they share certain rituals and traditions such as the concept of brotherhood and a secret handshake.

Guan Yu was a general loyal to Liu Bei, a warlord in the late Eastern Han dynasty who founded the state of Shu Han and became its first ruler. Guan played a significant role in the events which led to the collapse of the Eastern Han dynasty and the establishment of the state of Shu Han in the Three Kingdoms period. He is regarded by the

---

[58] "Sun Yat-Sen." Wikipedia. Wikimedia Foundation.

xxvii. Members of the Chinese Freemasons, Vernon, British Columbia, 1926

Hongmen as someone who embodies righteousness, patriotism, and loyalty.[59]

At the beginning of the Second Sino-Japanese War there was a significant increase in the number of Chinese Freemasons. Initially, the Japanese did not bother with these men, but as the war wore on, they began investigating Freemasonry in Shanghai and harassing the prominent members, who were then taken into custody for several weeks. Gradually, it became increasingly difficult for the Chinese lodges to operate. Although Hong Kong fell to the Japanese on December 1941 several lodges managed to meet informally in POW camps under dangerous conditions.

When the Japanese occupation ended the lodges in China and Hong Kong were revived, and there was a push to form the Grand Lodge of China. With the support of the British, the Grand Lodge was consecrated on March 18, 1949 at the Masonic Temple, Route Dufour, Shanghai.

With the establishment of the People's Republic of China the Grand Lodge of China ceased to function in Shanghai. It has operated in Taiwan since that time, and currently has 10 lodges with 750 members. Additionally, many of the other lodges located on mainland China transferred their warrants to Hong Kong as it was still under British

---

[59] "Guan Yu." Wikipedia. Wikimedia Foundation. https://en.wikipedia.org/wiki/Guan_Yu.

rule, and countless Chinese Freemasons followed the Nationalist government to Taiwan.[60]

Following the overthrow of the Qing dynasty in 1911, the Hongmen (Chinese Freemasons) in China diverged into various smaller groups. Some turned to illegal activities, thus giving birth to the modern *Triads*, a branch of the Chinese transnational organized crime syndicates.[61]

The Triads were a secret society established in Hong Kong, Macau, and Taiwan between 1914 and 1939. The word Triad is derived from the Chinese word, 三合會 (*Sanhehui*), which means Three Harmonies Society. The Sanhehui branched off from the Tiandihui, the Society of the Heaven and the Earth (the predecessors of the modern Chinese Freemasons). These societies adopted the triangle as their emblem. The various emblems utilized by the societies also typically employed other decorative images such as swords or portraits of Guan Yu.

During the 19th century these secret societies served as a legitimate resource for Chinese immigrants living abroad. Hence, the group that had originally established branches in Hong Kong, Macau, and Taiwan spread out to many countries where a significant Chinese population existed. These countries included: the United States, Canada, Vietnam,

---

[60] "Freemasonry in China." Zetland Hall. https://zetlandhall.com/history/china.
[61] "Hongmen: The Chinese Freemason's history stretches back to mid-seventeenth century secret societies in Southern China." Grand Lodge of British Columbia and Yukon. http://freemasonry.bcy.ca/history/chinese_freemasons/index.html.

Korea, Japan, Singapore, the Philippines, Indonesia, Malaysia, Thailand, the United Kingdom, Belgium, the Netherlands, France, Spain, South Africa, Australia, Brazil, and New Zealand. However, the British government considered the Triads a criminal threat and the group was charged with violating British Colonial Law, convicted, and imprisoned in British colonies, such as Hong Kong and Singapore, where they had organized.

After World War II, there was a resurgence of Triad groups as anti-British sentiment grew. Consequently, gang violence increased substantially in some communities. Following Mao Zedong's campaigns to crackdown on criminal organizations, which were also seen as an opposition to his power as Chairman of the People's Republic of China, the remaining Triad members fled to Hong Kong. By the 1950s Hong Kong had an estimated three hundred thousand Triad members residing and operating in the territory.

Organized crime groups reestablished themselves in China after Mao passed away, but these groups were not actually associated with the Triads.[62]

The Triads and the Umbrella Revolution

In 2014, a series of protests, referred to as the Umbrella Revolution, took place in Hong Kong. It was called the Umbrella Revolution because the protestors utilized umbrellas as tools for peaceful resistance against the China-backed Hong Kong government. The

---

[62] "Tiandihui." Wikipedia. Wikimedia Foundation. https://en.wikipedia.org/wiki/Tiandihui.

protests were in response to the Standing Committee of the National People's Congress' (NPCSC) decision regarding the proposed reforms to the Hong Kong electoral system. The decision was viewed as highly restrictive and gave the Chinese Communist Party the opportunity to pre-screen Hong Kong Chief Executive candidates. The Triad gangs played a major part in helping to suppress the protestors and instigated counter riots and demonstrations.[63]

The protests, which began in September of 2014, were led by the Hong Kong Federation of Students and a Hong Kong pro-democracy student activist group called Scholarism. Joining the students were Reverend Chu Yiu-ming, Dr. Benny Tai Yiu-ting, and Chan Kin-man. These men had organized a civil disobedience campaign on March 27, 2013, with the purpose of pressuring the government into reforming the electoral system. The campaign was known as the Occupy Central with Love and Peace and called for the occupation of the region's central business district if such reforms were not made. The Occupy Central with Love and Peace had originally planned to launch its protest campaign on October 1, 2014, the National Day of the People's Republic of China.

On September 28, students and other members of the public demonstrated outside government headquarters, and some began to occupy several major city intersections. The key areas in Admiralty, Causeway Bay, and Mong Kok were occupied and remained closed off to traffic for 77 days. On any given day, the number of protesters

---

[63] "2014 Hong Kong protests." Wikipedia. Wikimedia Foundation.https://en.wikipedia.org/wiki/2014_Hong_Kong_protests.

swelled to more than a hundred thousand, overwhelming the police and causing containment issues.[64]

The police used violence and tear gas to repel the protestors. The Triad gangs also joined in, hiring people for HK$800 per day, many of whom were from the poor districts of Hong Kong, to join in anti-Occupy riots. Some of the gangsters went so far as to attack and intimidate the Occupy protestors. It was reported that approximately 200 gangsters from two major Triad groups, Sun Yee On and Wo Shing Wo, had infiltrated Occupy Central camps with unknown motives. The protests came to an end on December 14, 2014, with no changes being made to the Standing Committee of the National People's Congress' original decision. The founders of Occupy Central with Love and Peace surrendered to the police when the protests came to an end and the organization was disbanded.[65]

Freemasonry in Communist China

Today, Freemasonry is outlawed by the Chinese Communist Party. However, the China Zhi Gong Party, which owes its roots to the Hongmen, is frequently utilized by the government of People's Republic of China on occasions where an intermediary is required for establishing a rapport with certain foreign interests. For example, when a delegation of Paraguayan politicians visited Beijing in 2001 and met Li Peng, they were invited not by the government of the People's

---

[64] "Umbrella Movement." Wikipedia. Wikimedia Foundation. https://en.wikipedia.org/wiki/Umbrella_Movement.
[65] Wing Lo, T. "Securitizing the Colour Revolution: Assessing the Political Role of Triads in Hong Kong's Umbrella Movement ." Academic.oup.com. https://academic.oup.com/bjc/article/61/6/1521/6261040.

Republic of China nor the Communist Party, but by the China Zhi Gong Party.

In April of 2007, Wan Gang, Deputy Chair of the China Zhi Gong Party Central Committee, was appointed Technology Minister of China. This marked the first non-Communist Party ministerial appointment in China since the 1950s.[66]

---

[66] "China Zhi Gong Party." Wikipedia. Wikimedia Foundation. https://en.wikipedia.org/China_Zhi_Gong_Party.

xxviii. Umbrella Revolution, umbrellas in Causeway Bay (Photo by Doctor Ho)

Key Dates in Japanese History

Date:	Event:
1543	A Chinese ship was blown off course and landed on the island of Tanegashima, just south of Kyushu. Three Portuguese traders were on board: António Mota, Francisco Zeimoto, and Fernão Mendes Pinto. They were the first Europeans to set foot in Japan.
1549	The Jesuit missionary, Francis Xavier, arrived in Kyushu.
1592	Toyotomi Hideyoshi launched first invasion of Korea.
1597	Toyotomi Hideyoshi launched second invasion of Korea.
1600	Tokugawa Ieyasu won a decisive victory at the Battle of Sekigahara and ushered in 268 uninterrupted years of rule by the Tokugawa clan.
1633 - 1639	Tokugawa Iemitsu established the Sakoku (closed country) period barring all foreigners from entering Japan and preventing the Japanese from leaving the country. The only foreigners allowed in were the Dutch. Trade continued with China and Korea.
1637	The Christian-led Shimabara Rebellion began.
1779	A Dutch surgeon, scholar, merchant-trader, and ambassador named Isaac Titsingh (Dutch East India Company), was the first Freemason to visit Japan.
1833	The Great Tenpo famine began.
1853	Commodore Matthew C. Perry arrived in Japan with the American fleet.

1854	On March 31st, the Kanagawa Treaty (Japan–US Treaty of Peace and Amity) became the first treaty between the United States of America and the Tokugawa Shogunate. Signed under the threat of force, it effectively ended Japan's policy of national seclusion by opening the ports of Shimoda and Hakodate to American trade vessels. It also ensured the safety of American castaways and established the position of an American consul in Japan.
1863	Japanese government agreed to have British and French troops stationed in Yokohama.
1864	The Sphinx Lodge No. 263, arrived in Yokohama with a detachment of the British 20th Regiment. Amane Nishi and Mamichi Tsuda were the first Japanese to become Freemasons abroad. They were initiated in La Vertu Lodge No. 7 in Leyden.
1866	Yokohama Lodge No. 1092 was formed. Shortly thereafter, a total of six English and three Scottish lodges were formed in Japan (The members were all foreigners who contributed to the modernization of Japan).
1867	Tokugawa Yoshinobu resigned.
1868	The Boshin War erupted and resulted in the end of the Shogunate and the restoration of imperial power. The Meiji period began. Shinto was adopted as the State Religion.
1877	The Satsuma Rebellion began.
1879	Arthur MacArthur, father of General Douglas MacArthur, was made a Master Mason in Magnolia Lodge No.60 at

		Little Rock, Arkansas.
1894		First Sino-Japanese War began.
1895		The island of Taiwan was ceded to Japan.
1902		The first Anglo-Japanese Alliance was signed in London by the representatives of Britain and Japan (Count Tadasu Hayashi). The alliance was renewed and expanded in scope twice, in 1905 and 1911, before its demise in 1921. It was officially terminated in 1923. Count Hayashi, was a career diplomat and later a statesman, stationed in England from 1900 to 1906. He became a Freemason while in England. He was initiated in Empire Lodge No. 2108 in February of 1903, passed to the Second Degree in March, and raised to the Third Degree in May.
1904		The Russo–Japanese War began.
1912		The Taisho period began.
1914 - 1918		Japan participated in World War I alongside the Allies.
1926		The Showa period began.
1936		January 14th, General Douglas MacArthur made *Mason at sight* at the Grand Lodge of the Philippines by Samuel Hawthorne. During the same ceremony, he was raised to *Master Mason*. On March 28th, General MacArthur became a 32nd degree Mason.

1937	Second Sino-Japanese War began.
1937	The government authorities began to crack down on the Freemasons.
1940	In the early 1940s the anti-Masonic movements intensified and all the lodges had to cease their operations.
1941	Japanese attacked Pearl Harbor in Hawaii as well as the Asian colonies of the United States, Great Britain, and the Netherlands, thus launching the Pacific War.
1945	Japan surrendered. The military occupation of Japan began led by the Supreme Commander of the Allied Powers, General Douglas MacArthur.
1947	General MacArthur raised to a 33rd degree Master Mason in the American Embassy of Japan.
1951	The San Francisco Peace Treaty was signed. General Douglas MacArthur was relieved by President Truman and replaced by General Matthew Ridgeway.
1952	The military occupation of Japan ended.

xxix. *Viscount Tadasu Hayashi (1850 – 1913) in circa 1902*

CHAPTER 6

Bushido, Shinto, and Freemasonry

Just as Confucianism and Taoism had become two of the most influential philosophies/ religious beliefs in China, Bushido and Shinto shaped Japanese society in a similar manner.

Bushido, or "the way of the warriors," is a Japanese collective term for the various codes of honor and ideals that dictated the samurai way of life. For the samurai, who comprised between 5 to 10 percent of the Japanese population, these ideals encompassed sincerity, frugality, loyalty, martial arts, and honor until death. Under the Bushido ideal, if a samurai failed to uphold his honor he could only regain it by performing *seppuku* (ritual suicide).

Bushido was, in a sense a part of a warrior's constant preparation for death. To die a good death, with one's honor intact, was the ultimate aim. The samurai were aware that their station in life, which involved killing, precluded them from any future rewards in the afterlife according to Buddhist teachings.

The samurai's moral values originated from Neo-Confucianism during times of peace in the Edo period (1603 to 1868). Neo-Confucianism originated in China during the Tang dynasty, a period generally regarded as a high point in Chinese civilization and a golden age of cosmopolitan culture. Neo-Confucianism reached Japan during the Kamakura period (1185–1333 AD), the period known for the emergence of the samurai, the warrior caste, and for the establishment of feudalism in Japan.[67]

When Japan entered into a period of peace after 1600, the once warring samurai class played a central role in the policing and administration of the country. Consequently, the Bushido literature of this period focused on the warrior class seeking a more general application of martial principles and experience.

There were notable differences in the Bushido theories which developed after Japan's modernization as opposed to those that were embraced by the samurai caste. Bushido in the prewar period was often emperor-centered and placed much greater value on the virtues of loyalty and self-sacrifice than did many Tokugawa-era interpretations. Bushido was used as a propaganda tool by the government and military, who doctored it to suit their needs.

Some authors have argued that modern Bushido emerged in the 1880s as a response to foreign stimuli, such as the English concept of chivalry. This relatively pacifistic Bushido was then appropriated and

---

[67] "Neo-Confucianism." Wikipedia. Wikimedia Foundation. https://en.wikipedia.org/wiki/Neo-Confucianism.

adapted by militarists and the government from the early 1900s onward as nationalism increased around the time of the Russo-Japanese War.

During pre-World War II and World War II, Bushido was used to encourage militarism in Japan, present war as purifying, and death as a duty. Bushido would provide a spiritual shield to let soldiers fight to the end.

As the war turned more in favor of the Allies, Japan proposed using organized suicide attacks (*kamikaze*) as a last ditch effort to obtaining a favorable concession. This proposal met resistance because although Bushido called for a warrior to always be aware of death, they were not to view it as the sole end. Nonetheless, the desperate situation brought about acceptance and such attacks were acclaimed as the true spirit of Bushido.[68]

Similarly, Shinto also underwent an alteration process during the pre-war period and helped shape the Japanese mindset during the Pacific War.

The name *Shinto* (Way of the Gods) was originally adopted from the Chinese word *Shendao* (神道), in which the kanji 神 (Shen) meant *kami* (spirit/ deity) and 道 (Dao) meant *michi* (philosophical path or study). Hence, Shinto is also known as *kami-no-michi* in Japan.

---

[68] "Bushido." Wikipedia. Wikimedia Foundation. https://en.wikipedia.org/wiki/Bushido.

The earliest Shinto practices were first recorded and codified in the 8th century; however, Shinto represented a collection of native beliefs and mythology rather than a unified religion in those early writings. There is no core sacred text associated with Shinto, such as the *Bible* in Christianity or the *Koran* in Islam. Instead, there are books of folklore and history that provide stories and background to many Shinto beliefs. One of these books is the *Kojiki* (*Records of Ancient Matters*). Dating back to the early 8th century, the work serves as the oldest existing chronicle of Japan. It was written by a Japanese nobleman, bureaucrat, and chronicler, Ono Yasumaro, upon the request of Empress Genmei, the 43rd monarch of Japan who ruled from 707 until 715. The book is a collection of myths detailing the origin of Japan and its spirits/deities, which were later appropriated for Shinto practices. It established the Japanese imperial family as the foundation of Japanese culture, and as descendants of *Amaterasu Omikami* (the most important deity of the Shinto religion and ruler of *Takama no Hara*, the domain of the kami or spirits.)

The second oldest book of classical Japanese history which influenced Shinto is known as the *Nihon Shoki* (sometimes translated as *The Chronicles of Japan*). It was completed in 720 AD under the editorial supervision of Prince Toneri with Ono Yasumaro's assistance. It was more elaborate and detailed than the *Kojiki*, and instrumental in creating a structured system of government, foreign policy, religious hierarchy, and domestic social order.

When Buddhism was introduced in Japan during the Asuka period (6th century), rather than abandoning their old belief system the Japanese attempted to merge the two. What emerged was *Shinbutsushugo*, which served as Japan's only organized religion until the Meiji period. Although the old system and Buddhism never quite fused they remained linked, which continues through present day.

Beginning in 1868, the new Meiji government issued a series of laws which formally separated Buddhism and Shinto. This was also the time when Shinto elements came under state influence and control as the government systematically used shrine worship as a major force for mobilizing imperial loyalties on behalf of building a modern nation. The Meiji Restoration reasserted the importance of the emperor and the ancient chronicles and established the Empire of Japan. Thus, State Shinto was instituted as a means for achieving unification around the emperor as the process of modernization was undertaken with remarkable speed. The psychological shock of the appearance of Commodore Perry's black ships and the subsequent collapse of the Shogunate had convinced many Japanese that the nation needed to unify in order to resist colonization by outside forces.

In 1871, the *Jingikan* (Ministry of Rites) was established, and priests were officially nominated and organized by the government. They were charged with instructing the youth on Shinto theology based on the dogma of the divinity of Japan's national origins and its emperor. However, the Japanese people did not accept this propaganda and the Ministry was dissolved in the mid-1870s.

Although the government sponsorship of shrines declined, Japanese nationalism remained closely linked to the legends of foundation and emperors. The government argued that Shinto was a non-religious, moral tradition and patriotic practice. The *Imperial Rescript on Education* was issued in 1890, which required students to ritually recite an oath to offer themselves courteously to the State and to do all they could to protect the imperial family. By 1940, Shinto priests risked persecution for performing traditionally religious Shinto ceremonies.

All of this came to an abrupt end following Japan's surrender in August of 1945. On December 15, 1945, during the Allied Occupation of Japan, the Supreme Commander for the Allied Powers, General Douglas MacArthur, issued the Shinto Directive. Its purpose was to abolish government support for the Shinto religion. The Allies believed that it had been a major contributor to Japan's nationalistic and militant culture and led to Japan's participation in World War II. The purpose of the directive was likely based on the ideas of freedom of religion and the separation of church and state, both of which are included in the Constitution of the United States, although the lines of separation have become somewhat blurred in recent years.

On January 1, 1946, Emperor Hirohito, after meeting with General MacArthur, issued the *Ningen-sengen* (The Humanity Declaration). The Ningen-sengen was an imperial rescript incorporated into the emperor's New Year's statement in which the emperor denied the concept of being an *akitsumikami* (a deity in human form). This declaration would eventually lead to the proclamation of the new Constitution, under which the emperor became the symbol of Japan and of the unity of the people.

Today, Shinto is the traditional religion of Japan and stands apart from the foreign religions such as Christianity, Buddhism, and Islam, which coexist in the country, albeit to a lesser degree. Shinto focuses on a set of ritual practices that have to be diligently carried out to establish a connection between present-day Japan and its ancient past. Nearly 80 percent of the population of Japan participates in Shinto practices or rituals, but only a small percentage of these individuals actually identify themselves as Shintoists. Most of the Japanese attend Shinto shrines and implore kami without belonging to an institutional Shinto religion. Actually, less than 40 percent of the population of Japan currently identifies with an organized religion. Of those who do, approximately 35 percent claim to be Buddhists, while 3 to 4 percent are members of Shinto sects and religions derived from it. To date, 90,000 Shinto shrines and 79,000 Shinto priests can be found in Japan.[69]

Freemasonry Gains a Foothold in Japan

As Japan came under many foreign influences, which subsequently led to the country's modernization, history paved the path for another foreign element to gain a foothold in a country that had once isolated itself from the West. Freemasonry had spread quickly both in Europe and America; therefore, it was just a question of time before it spread to Japan as well.

---

[69] "Guide to Shinto Shrines in Japan - Features and Styles." Guide to Shinto Shrines in Japan - Features and Styles | Asia Highlights.
https://www.asiahighlights.com/japan/guide-to-shinto-shrines.

Isaac Titsingh

It is believed that the first Freemason to visit Japan was a Dutch surgeon, scholar, merchant-trader, and ambassador named Isaac Titsingh (January 10, 1745 - February 12, 1812). Titsingh was initiated as a Freemason in Batavia in 1772. Freemasons belonging to the Dutch East India Company and stationed in Dejima or Canton prior to 1800 had often been initiated in or were members of La Fidèle Sincérité (established 1771) and Lodge La Vertueuse (established in 1769) in Batavia, the capital city of the Dutch East Indies (modern day Jakarta in Indonesia).

Freemasonry was not uncommon in the Netherlands. The first Dutch lodge was founded in The Hague in 1734, followed by a Grand Lodge in 1735. During the 18th and 19th centuries, several hundred lodges were founded in the Netherlands and its overseas trading posts.

The founding of the overseas lodges primarily served to spread Freemasonry across the globe and provide additional funds for the grand lodges. Between 1757 and 1837 dozens of Dutch lodges were established in India, Ceylon, Java, Malacca, and Japan; while Dutch Freemasons were also members of an international lodge in Canton, China.

Titsingh was a senior official of the Dutch East India Company, officially known as the Verenigde Oostindische Compagnie (VOC). He, along with men like Archibald Mesterton, Pieter Romberg, Claes Grill, Andreas Everardus van Braam Houckgeest, and Joost Schouten served as important links in the Masonic network between the

Netherlands and Southeast Asia. The VOC was so powerful that it possessed pseudo-governmental powers, which included the ability to wage war, imprison and execute convicts, negotiate treaties, strike its own coins, and establish colonies. Therefore, the VOC played a crucial role in the business, military, political, and the exploratory maritime history of the world.

A comparison of the enlistment records of the Dutch East India Company with the membership lists of lodges in India, Ceylon, and Canton reveals that between 1757 and 1800, 20 to 30 percent of the company's high ranking officers were Freemasons.

Isaac Titsingh traveled to Japan three times: in 1779, 1781, and 1784. As the head of the Dutch trading post in Nagasaki, he formed lasting friendships with influential Japanese citizens and scholars.

Commodore Matthew C. Perry

What made Japan so attractive to the United States and European powers was its abundant supply of gold and silver. The West had been syphoning off these riches from South America, Africa, and Asia; and Japan and Thailand were the only two countries left untouched in the struggle to amass the spoils of manifest destiny.

Japan had enjoyed 250 years of peace under the Shogun's regime and lacked the weapons for killing large masses of people. This left her vulnerable to American and European pirates who attacked from the sea. The country was also defenseless against the importation of opium that had brought down the Qing dynasty in China and was now making its way into Japan.

On July 29, 1858, the Shogunate or Bakufu was forced to sign the Treaty of Amity and Commerce drawn up by Townsend Harris, the first American envoy to Japan. Article 4 of the Treaty stipulated that Japan was to permit the import of 1.8 kilograms (four pounds) of opium. This treaty was signed four years after Commodore Perry visited Japan a second time.

Commodore Matthew Calbraith Perry, a Freemason and member of The Holland Lodge No. 8 in New York since 1819, had commanded ships in several wars including the War of 1812 and the Mexican-American War of 1846.

In 1852, United States President Millard Fillmore ordered Perry to force open Japanese ports to American trade—through the use of gunboat diplomacy if necessary. Gunboat diplomacy was a term that came into existence during the 19th century period of Western imperialism. The United States and Britain (primarily) would use their naval superiority to intimidate less powerful nations into granting concessions favorable to the Western powers.

Ironically, Fillmore was staunchly opposed to Freemasonry and had been elected to the New York state legislature in 1828 on the anti-Masonic ticket.

Perry left from Norfolk, Virginia to Japan on November 24, 1852. He arrived in Naha (Okinawa) on May 17 of the following year and demanded an audience with the Ryukyuan ruler Sho Tai at Shuri Castle. Armed with promises that the Ryukyuan Kingdom would be opened to trade with the United States, he journeyed to the Ogasawara Islands (also known as the Bonin Islands) located 620 miles (1,000 kilometers) south of Edo (Tokyo). In the Ogasawara Islands Perry met with the local inhabitants and purchased a plot of land from them.

On July 8, 1853, Perry reached Uraga, a town in modern-day Kanagawa prefecture, located at the northern end of the Uraga Channel, a waterway connecting Edo Bay (Tokyo Bay) to the Sagami Gulf. He ordered his ships to sail toward Edo and turn their guns toward Uraga. He attempted to intimidate the Japanese by commanding his ships to fire blank shots. He landed in Kurihama (modern-day Yokosuka) on July 14, 1853, and presented the Japanese delegation with a letter which stated that the Americans would destroy them if they chose to fight. Perry departed for Hong Kong after informing the delegation that he would return the following year to hear Japan's response.

Commodore Perry returned to Japan on February 13, 1854, six months earlier than expected, with ten ships and 1,600 men. His intention was to apply even more pressure on the Japanese to agree to his terms. Perry and his crew were initially met with resistance upon their return however, Perry was permitted to set foot on Japanese soil once again on March 8, 1854. On March 31, 1854, the Convention of Kanagawa was signed.

xxx. Commodore Matthew Calbraith Perry

When Perry returned to the United States in 1855, he was awarded $20,000 ($682,317 in 2022) in appreciation of his accomplishments in Japan.[70]

Thomas Blake Glover

Upon examining Japan's evolution from a closed country to a free-trading, modern nation, it becomes apparent that the traders, many of whom were associated with Freemasonry, played a crucial role. One trader in particular was highly instrumental in helping to cast off the age of feudalism and usher in the modern age. His name was Thomas Blake Glover.

Thomas Glover was a Scottish trader who provided arms and assistance to the anti-Tokugawa Choshu clan through his Nagasaki-based trading company. Sakamoto Ryoma, a prominent figure in the movement to overthrow the Tokugawa Shogunate and a close friend of Glover's, purchased arms with funds provided by the Satsuma clan for the venture. It was through his association with such men as Sakamoto Ryoma, that Thomas Glover was able to influence the future direction Japan was to take.

Operating as an agent of the Chinese-based Jardine, Matheson & Company, he competed in 1863-1864 with the American Eugene Van Reed, a Freemason and a merchant with the Yokohama branch of the Canton-based Augustine Heard & Company, for privileged status in

---

[70] "World Civilizations II (HIS102) – Biel." From the Edo Period to Meiji Restoration in Japan | World Civilizations II (HIS102) – Biel.
https://courses.lumenlearning.com/suny-fmcc-worldcivilization2/chapter/from-the-edo-period-to-meiji-restoration-in-japan/.

xxxi. Sakamoto Ryoma

trade with the Satsuma clan. (Van Reed passed away in 1873 and was buried in the Masonic Cemetery at the foot of Lone Mountain, San Francisco, California.)

Glover had been working as a shipping clerk at the age of 16 when he garnered the attention of the prominent trading company, Jardine Matheson Far Eastern, founded in Canton in 1832 by two Scotsmen William Jardine and James Matheson. The company with ostensible Masonic ties, traded in opium, cotton, tea, silk, and a variety of other goods, controlling around half of China's foreign trade.

At the end of the First Opium War (1839 – 42), the island of Hong Kong was ceded to the British by the Qing dynasty of China. In 1844 Jardine, Matheson & Co. established its head office in Hong Kong and proceeded to expand all along the China Coast. New offices were also opened in the trading centers of Fuzhou and Tianjin. The company promoted railways and other much needed infrastructure projects in China and founded banks and insurance companies. This helped propel the country towards modernization. Further growth occurred in the early decades of the 20th century as the company embarked upon new cold storage, packing, and brewing businesses. The firm also operated the largest cotton spinning facilities in Shanghai.[71]

Glover was hired by Jardine, Matheson & Co. and posted to Shanghai soon after. He arrived as the Second Opium War was ravaging China and performed well for two years, selling opium to local middlemen,

---

[71] "History of Jardine Matheson & Co.." Wikipedia. Wikimedia Foundation. https://en.wikipedia.org/wiki/History_of_Jardine_Matheson_%26_Co.

and trading in silks, tea, and guns. In doing so, Glover managed to obtain the clout to command his own cut of the deals he was negotiating for his employer. When Japan opened up for foreign traders, Glover saw an opportunity to prosper further.

He arrived in Nagasaki in 1859 and proceeded to build up a mini real estate empire in Dejima, where he had taken up residence. In 1861, he founded the Glover Trading Co. (*Guraba-Shokei*) to deal illegally—in light of a commerce treaty signed in 1858 between Britain and the Shogunate—in ships and weapons with the rebellious Satsuma and Chosu clans in Kyushu and the Tosa clan from Shikoku. Glover managed to prosper significantly by playing each side against the other and becoming Kyushu's biggest arms dealer.

Glover was also involved in helping to smuggle young samurai from the Choshu (the Choshu Five) and Satsuma (Godai Tomoatsu) clans to study abroad. This was in direct violation of Tokugawa's *Sakoku* policy. The young men traveled to England aboard Jardine Matheson ships.

The Choshu Five traveled to England in 1863 to study at University College, London, and were the first of many successive groups to travel overseas during the late *Bakumatsu* (the time period between the arrival of Commodore Matthew Perry in 1853 and the fall of the Tokugawa Shogunate in 1868) and early Meiji periods. All five later rose to prominent positions in Japanese political and civil life.

xxxii. Thomas Blake Glover, recipient of the Order of the Rising Sun

xxxiii. Glover with Iwasaki Yanosuke, the brother of the founder of Mitsubishi, circa 1900

It was during the Bakumatsu period (1863) that Thomas Blake Glover's house in Nagasaki was completed. Located on the Minamiyamate hillside overlooking Nagasaki Harbor, the house served as the venue for Glover's meetings with rebel samurai from the Choshu and Satsuma clans. The house still stands and is surrounded by a park known as Glover Garden. The stone gate from the Nagasaki Lodge No. 710 is preserved in Glover Garden.

Nagasaki Lodge No. 710 was inaugurated at No. 50 Oura on October 5, 1885. It was founded by Scotsman, John Fulton Calder, who served as the lodge's first Master. The lodge was moved to a new building at No. 47 Oura in June of 1887. In 1911, most of Nagasaki's foreign community had transferred its businesses to the Kobe-Osaka area, which negatively impacted the membership of the lodge. Consequently, Nagasaki Lodge No. 710 was forced to surrender its charter and close its doors. Today, the graves of several former Freemasons can be found in Nagasaki's international cemeteries. One of those Freemasons is John Fulton Calder, who is buried at the Sakamoto International Cemetery in Nagasaki.[72]

---

[72] Calder, John Fulton." Meiji-era Portraits. http://meiji-portraits.de/meiji_c.html#CALDERJohnFulton.

xxxiv. The Choshu Five in 1863

xxxv. Glover House known as Ipponmatsu (Single Pine Tree) from a drawing of 1863. The tree was chopped down in the early 1900s

In 1865 Glover spurred the Satsuma-Choshu-Britain summit to forge a rapport between the clans—which in turn encouraged the British government not to step in to stop their rebellion or prevent the sale of arms. Satsuma and Choshu had historically been irreconcilable enemies, but Sakamoto Ryoma had negotiated a secret alliance between the military leaders of the two provinces (The Satcho Alliance). The Satcho Alliance was otherwise known as the Satsuma-Choshu Alliance and was an abbreviation combining the names of the Satsuma and Choshu clans.

The alliance was forged in 1866 between Saigo Takamori and Okubo Toshimichi, the military leaders of Satsuma, and Katsura Kogoro of Choshu in an effort to combine their efforts to restore Imperial rule and

xxxvi. Gate of the former Nagasaki Lodge No. 710 located in Glover Garden

overthrow the Tokugawa Shogunate. The Imperial army which finally overthrew the Shogunate following the Boshin War of 1867, consisted of samurai from the Satcho Alliance. Men from the two clans subsequently dominated the new Meiji government.

With the dawn of the new Meiji era, Japan threw her doors wide open for trade with the world. The market for Glover's weaponry soon became saturated as the new government assumed sole control of acquisitions. Glover's direct political influence waned, but his connectedness and his experience brokering the building and sale of ocean-going ships guaranteed a favorable role for him under the new regime.

As the demand for steamships increased so did the demand for coal. In 1868, Glover turned to developing the Takashima coal mine located on an island near Nagasaki. The Takashima mine became the first mine in Japan to employ Western methods of mining. Unfortunately, bad luck and poor accounting methods forced Glover to eventually sell his stake in the mine. Mitsubishi purchased the mine in 1881 and allowed Glover to stay on as its manager.

The Mitsubishi conglomerate was originally the Tosa clan's Tsukumo Trading Company. Iwasaki Yataro, who had been working for the Tosa government, leased the trading rights for the company and became its president in March of 1870. In 1871, the company, which had earlier been known as Mitsukawa Shokai and then Mitsubishi Shokai, was renamed Mitsubishi Steamship Company.

Iwasaki Yataro was the great grandson of a Tosa samurai who had sold his family's samurai status to satisfy his debts. Through his association with Yoshida Toyo, a reformer and samurai of the Tosa clan, Iwasaki managed to secure a job as a clerk for the Tosa government. He was promoted to the top position at the Tosa clan's trading office in Nagasaki and managed to buy back his family's samurai status.

While in the employ of the Tosa government, Iwasaki also supported the activities of the Kaientai. The Kaientai was a private navy and trading company founded by Sakamoto Ryoma. It was through his involvement with the Kaientai that Iwasaki first met Sakamoto. The two men shared a similar awareness of a larger world and a focus on modernizing Japan.[73]

Iwasaki Yataro and his younger brother, Yanosuke, who became Mitsubishi's second president after his brother's death, had forged an enduring friendship with Glover. It was through this bond with Glover that the older brother was able to obtain ships and armaments for the Tosa clan.

In 1885 Glover brokered a deal establishing the Japan Brewery Company Limited, the forerunner to Kirin Brewery. The company was incorporated in Hong Kong in the name of W.H. Talbot and E.H. Abbott with financial backing provided by a group of Japanese investors including Iwasaki Yanosuke.

Glover also negotiated other deals bringing mostly Scottish engineers to mid-Meiji era projects that included town planning, lighthouse-building, and railway construction. In this way Glover contributed immensely to the industrialization and modernization of Japan. Emperor Meiji awarded Glover the Order of the Rising Sun in 1908 in recognition of his contributions.[74]

John Fulton Calder

Among the engineers who arrived in Japan with Glover's intervention was a man named John Fulton Calder, Freemason and the founder of

---

[73] "Vol. 6 Yataro & Ryoma-Sharing a Common Dream." Mitsubishi Corporation. www.mitsubishicorp.com/jp/en/mclibrary/roots/vol06/.
[74] "Thomas Glover." 三菱グループサイト, https://www.mitsubishi.com/en/profile/history/series/thomas/.

Nagasaki Lodge No. 710.

Calder was born in Midlothian, Scotland and arrived in Nagasaki in 1867. He initially worked for C. Cherry & Company, Boiler Makers and Blacksmiths, before joining the engineering firm of Boyd & Co. located at Nos. 48 - 49 Oura. Boyd & Co. was purchased by Mitsubishi Mail Steamship Company in 1879. Calder continued to work for them until 1881, after which time he transitioned to Osaka Iron Works. In 1884 Calder returned to Nagasaki and began work as the manager of Mitsubishi Shipyard and Engine Works. He remained with the firm until his death on May 23, 1892.[75]

The Freemasons in Yokohama

Once Japan had concluded treaties with the Western powers and opened up her ports for foreign trade, the resulting unequal treaties and rampant inflation threw the country into turmoil and brought about the rise of a new political philosophy and social movement known as "*sonno joi*" (Revere the emperor, expel the barbarians). Since the Shogunate had signed the treaties opening up the country to foreign trade and its subsequent influences, numerous dissatisfied samurai adopted this slogan as they attempted to overthrow the Bakufu.

As a result, assaults on foreigners in Japan became commonplace causing the foreign powers to lodge strong protests. The Japanese government acquiesced to the foreigners' demands and agreed to have British and French troops stationed in Yokohama in 1863. The foreign

---

[75] Calder, John Fulton." Meiji-era Portraits.

troops brought Freemasonry with them to Japan.

The Sphinx Lodge No. 263 came to Japan with a detachment of the British 20th Regiment; they arrived in Yokohama in 1864. The lodge held meetings and admitted civilian members, but since it was a military lodge it could not sustain its operation. The lodge held its last meeting in March of 1866.

Left without a lodge, the Freemasons living in Yokohama petitioned the United Grand Lodge of England. They were granted the right to establish a lodge and thus the Yokohama Lodge No. 1092 was formed and held its first regular meeting on June 26, 1866. Shortly thereafter, a total of six English and three Scottish lodges were formed in Japan. The members were all foreigners who contributed to the modernization of Japan. Among the members were a German merchant active in the development of Kobe, a British diplomat/scholar of Japanese literature whose works introduced Japan to the English-speaking world, and a British journalist, J.R. Black, who published an English-language newspaper, the *Japan Gazette*, and two Japanese newspapers, the *Nisshin Shinjishi* and *Bankoku Shimbun*. Black was the father of Japan's first foreign-born rakugo storyteller, Henry James Black whose stage name was Kairakutei Black I.

The First Japanese Freemasons

The first Japanese nationals to be initiated into the craft were two scholars: Nishi Amane (1829-1897) and Tsuda Mamichi (1829-1903). Both men studied at Leiden University in the Netherlands from 1862 to 1865 under Professor Simon Vissering. The professor was also a

xxxvii. J.R. Black

Freemason. Nishi was initiated in Loge La Vertu in Leiden in October of 1864. La Vertu is one of the oldest masonic temples in the Netherlands. Tsuda was initiated in November of 1864. Eventually, other Japanese men became Freemasons while traveling abroad including Count Hayashi Tadasu (1850-1913), a career diplomat and statesman, who became a Freemason while stationed in England from 1900 to 1906.

As with the Freemasons in other countries that had come before them, the Japanese Freemasons were highly influential individuals. They

xxxviii. Nishi Amane by Takahashi Yuichi 1893

adhered to the common Masonic belief that each man has responsibilities to improve himself and to help make the world a better place. They did this by helping propel Japan into the modern age.

Nishi Amane was a tireless advocate of using Western civilization as a role model for Japan's modernization and stressed the need to evolve without losing the Japanese character. He was born in modern day Shimane prefecture in 1829 and was the son of a samurai physician who practiced Chinese medicine. He was sent to Edo (Tokyo) in 1853 to learn *Rangaku* (Dutch learning which included studying the Dutch language and Western knowledge in a wide variety of disciplines) with the intent of becoming an interpreter for conducting business with the West through Dutch traders based in Dejima and Nagasaki.

In response to increased pressure to end the national isolation policy, the Shogunate decided to send Nishi Amane and Tsuda Mamichi to the Netherlands to learn the western concepts of political science, constitutional law, and economics. The two men left Japan in 1863 with Dutch physician, Dr. J. L. C. Pompe van Meerdervoort, who had set up the first teaching hospital for Western medicine in Nagasaki.

Upon their arrival in the Netherlands, they were placed in the care of Professor Vissering, who taught political economy, statistics, and diplomatic history at Leiden University. The professor felt that the students' strong desire for knowledge would make them likely future participants in Japan's modernization.

Nishi returned to Japan in 1865 and became an active participant in the

Meiji Restoration. He vigorously promoted contact with the West and Western intellectualism because he feared that in the long run a domestic resistance to modernization and change would be more destructive to Japan than the repercussions resulting from Japan's contact with the West.

Nishi published an encyclopedia called, *The Hyakugaku Renkan*, based on the French encyclopedia published by Auguste Comte. In it, Nishi classified and categorized the intellectual realms of Western civilization. He also promoted the concept that learning should not just be for sake of learning, as that does not serve a greater purpose.

Nishi was one of the ten original members of the Meiji Six Society (the Meirokusha), founded in 1874 (Japan's first scholarly society, focused solely on academics; not politics). The society was devoted to the education and enlightenment of the people because its members believed Japan needed an enlightened populace in order to understand and live up to its political and moral responsibilities as a modern nation.

In his next publication, *Jinsei Sampo Setsu* (1875), he urged all Japanese to seek the goals of health, knowledge and wealth, or what he called the "three treasures," in place of Confucian subservience and frugality. Moreover, Nishi believed that the Japanese government should be responsible for promoting the pursuit of these three treasures in society, and as a result Japan would be strengthened politically and socially without the intervention of Western rule or governmental tactics.

While working at the Ministry of Military Affairs, Nishi helped in drafting the *Conscription Ordinance of 1873*. This law introduced universal conscription and laid the foundation for the Imperial Japanese Army. In his lectures to the military, he emphasized discipline and obedience over seniority and hierarchy. These ideals were incorporated into the subsequent *Imperial Rescript to Soldiers and Sailors* in 1882.

In 1890, Nishi became a member of the House of Peers of the Diet of Japan after the Japanese general election.

Tsuda Mamichi was a Japanese statesman, legal scholar, and one of the founding members of the Meirokusha (The Meiji Six Society) along with Nishi Amane.

Born to a local samurai family in modern day Okayama prefecture, he studied Rangaku and military science. He later became an assistant to an instructor at the *Bansho Shirabesho* (Institute for the Study of Barbarian Books). This Japanese institute was charged with the translation and study of foreign books and publications in the late Edo period.

Tsuda returned to Japan in 1868 after completing his studies at Leiden University and published the translated lectures of Professor Vissering known as the *Taisei Kokuhoron* in 1868. These lectures dealt with the topic of Western law. The *Taisei Kokuhoron* was the first such book in Japanese on the topic. He was later recruited by the Meiji government to help in the first codification of Japanese laws.

xxxix. Tsuda Mamichi

Tsuda served in the Chamber of Elders and in the House of Peers of the Diet of Japan after the Japanese general election in 1890.

Count Hayashi Tadasu, who was briefly discussed earlier, was a Japanese diplomat and perhaps best known for negotiating the Anglo-Japanese Alliance of 1902.

Born in modern day Chiba prefecture, Hayashi was the son of a physician who practiced Dutch medicine, Sato Taizen. He was adopted by another physician, Hayashi Dokai, who was employed in the service of the Tokugawa Shogunate.

Hayashi attended the Hepburn Academy in Yokohama where he learned English. In 1866 he was among fourteen students selected by the Tokugawa government to study in England at both University College School and King's College London.

He returned to Japan in 1868 in the midst of the Boshin War and joined a short-lived rebellion of Tokugawa loyalists led by Enomoto Takeaki.

He was captured by Imperial forces and imprisoned in Yokohama.

Hayashi was released in 1871 and recruited by the Meiji government as an interpreter for Iwakura Tomomi during his mission to Europe and the United States from 1871 to 1873.

Upon his return to Japan, Hayashi worked at the Ministry of Public Works. He was later appointed governor of Kagawa prefecture and then of Hyogo prefecture. In 1891 he became the Vice Minister for Foreign Affairs and was elevated to the title of Baron (*Danshaku*) in 1895.

Hayashi actively participated in the conclusion of the Treaty of Shimonoseki that ended the Sino-Japanese War (1894–95). After the war he served successively as ambassador to China and minister to Russia. In 1899 he became ambassador to England, where he achieved his greatest diplomatic triumph. Alarmed by the expansion of Russian power in the Far East, he was instrumental in concluding the Anglo-Japanese Alliance (1902); it remained a pillar of Japanese foreign policy for the next twenty years. The alliance with Great Britain protected Japan from possible intervention of other European powers during its war with Russia in 1904–05. After the Russo-Japanese War, Hayashi served as Minister for Foreign Affairs from 1906 to 1908.

As these progressive individuals helped usher in Japan's modern age they also inadvertently contributed to a more militaristic society. Without question, the military had a strong influence on Japanese society starting with the Meiji Restoration as almost all of the Meiji leaders were former samurai or descendants of samurai. The early Meiji government embraced the Western model of modernization but at the same time saw Japan being threatened by Western imperialism. Growing domestic issues also called for a strong military. The government was threatened by internal revolts such as the Saga Rebellion, the Satsuma Rebellion, and numerous rural peasant uprisings. Consequently, the Meiji leadership took the necessary steps to strengthen Japan's economic and industrial foundations, so that a strong military could be built to defend Japan against outside powers.

The Anti-Masonic Movement

As Japan became more militaristic and further dominated by ultranationalist groups during the late 1930s, the situation deteriorated for the Freemasons in Japan. The government began cracking down on the fraternity as nationalism increased and anti-foreign sentiment began to mount, particularly after the outbreak of the Second Sino-Japanese War in 1937.

The anti-Masonic movement in Japan was further aided by one of the most active Catholic writers of the Meiji era, Father F. Ligneul, of the Société des Missions étrangères de Paris (Society of Foreign Missions of Paris). The Société was a Roman Catholic missionary organization established in 1658. It was not a religious institute, but an organization of secular priests and lay persons dedicated to missionary work in foreign lands.

Father Ligneul had launched the first anti-Masonic movement in March of 1900 by publishing a book entitled *Himitsu Kessha* (Secret Society). The book, which was reprinted in 1934, consisted of thirty-two chapters devoted to a variety of subjects relating to Freemasonry. Father Ligneul attacked Freemasonry by stating, "It advocates absolute freedom and equality of the people by completely destroying the present society and all of its systems ... Its ultimate goal is based on destructionism." Ligneul came to Japan in 1880 and was actively engaged in missionary work. He left the country in 1912.

While Father Ligneul had instigated anti-Masonic sentiments in Japan, religious groups in general were not among the principal foes of the Freemasons in Japan. In fact, anti-Semitism was the main driving force of anti-Masonic movements at the time.

Although Japan had a very limited number of Jews among its population, anti-Semitism had long been present in the country. By the middle of 1917, Japan had established a lucrative trade with the eastern ports in Russia. A number of Japanese companies had set up branch offices in Eastern Siberia and Manchuria, and many Japanese had become semi-permanent residents in those regions. The Bolshevik Revolution of 1917 was of great concern for Japan, and in 1918 she began sending troops to Siberia to join the Allied forces. As the Japanese troops advanced into Siberia their officers came into contact with White Russian officers who they supported. The White Russian officers vehemently criticized both the Bolsheviks and the Jews and provided their Japanese counterparts with anti-Semitic publications including *The Protocols of the Learned Elders of Zion*.

Judaic-Masonic Conspiracy Theories

The Protocols is an anti-Semitic, fabricated text alleging the existence of a Jewish plan for global domination. The forgery was first published in Russia in 1903, then translated into multiple languages and disseminated internationally in the early part of the 20th century. According to the claims made by some of its publishers, *The Protocols* documents the minutes of a late 19th century meeting in which Jewish leaders discussed their goal of global Jewish domination by subverting the morals of Gentiles and by controlling the press and the world's economies.

The first Japanese pamphlet quoting from *The Protocols* surfaced in 1919 in Vladivostok, a major Pacific port city in Russia near the borders with China and North Korea. Since then, *The Protocols* have been republished many times and most anti-Masonic writers in Japan have based their Judaic-Masonic conspiracy theories on these writings. Subsequently, anti-Semitic and anti-Masonic activities were launched by the military forces, educators, and the mass media.

During a meeting of nationalistic sociology professors at the Tokyo Imperial University on June 28, 1921, an assistant professor of the literature department, launched an attack on Freemasonry. He said it was a dangerous, subversive, secret society. Marshal Hisaichi Terauchi, Lt. General Nobutaka Shioten, and other high ranking Army officials also fueled the anti-Masonic and anti-Semitic movements. They declared that it was a crime for any Army officials to be Freemasons.

In 1938, a Japanese representative to the *Welt-Dienst* (German for World-Service) Congress stated on behalf of Japan, "Judeo-Masonry is forcing the Chinese to turn China into a spearhead for an attack on Japan, and thereby forcing Japan to defend herself against this threat. Japan is at war not with China but with Freemasonry (Tiandihui), represented by General Chiang Kai-shek, the successor of his master, the Freemason Sun Yat-sen."[76]

World-Service (also known as the International Correspondence for Enlightenment on the Jewish Question) was an international National Socialist news agency founded on December 1, 1933 in Erfurt, Germany by Ulrich Fleischhauer. The agency issued news bulletins in eight languages and sponsored the international conference of the Pan-Aryan Anti-Jewish Union from 1936 to 1938.

In 1940 all political parties were ordered to dissolve into the Imperial Rule Assistance Association, forming a one-party state based on totalitarian values. By the spring of 1940, Masonic activities in Japan had slowed down considerably. Many members had left the country. In the early 1940s there was an intensification of anti-Masonic movements. In November of 1941 the last Masonic meeting was held in Japan until after the war. Articles were published in newspapers as a warning to Freemasons and described what would happen to them if they did not get out of Japan.

Murayama Tamotsu, the first Japanese to be raised to the Degree of Master Mason in post-war Japan, recalled a story about an event on December 8, 1941 when the police came to arrest him. They asked him if he had been associated with any secret organizations attempting to overthrow the Japanese government and specifically mentioned the Freemasons. He was questioned because he was working at the Associated Press office in Tokyo and had been involved with the Boy

---

[76] Bessel, Paul M. "Bigotry and the Murder of Freemasonry." *Constitution*. November 1994. Bessel.org/naziart.htm.

xl. Murayama Tamotsu (Center)

Scouts. The Freemasons, the International Rotary Club, and Boy Scouts were banned in Japan. As a matter of fact, following the outbreak of the Pacific War the Japanese closed down all the Rotary Clubs in Japan and her territories. The Rotary Club was suspected to have conspired with the Freemasons against Japanese policies. It was said that the Boy Scout's pledge of brotherhood was derived from the Freemasons and therefore the organization was banned.

General Douglas MacArthur

After WWII, Masonic activities resumed in Japan. General Douglas MacArthur, the Supreme Commander of the Allies during the occupation of Japan and a Master Mason, was highly supportive of Masonic activities in Japan. Masonic lodges were once again formed in Japan by American soldiers during the occupation. At the time these lodges came under the jurisdiction of the Grand Lodge of the Philippines.

General MacArthur was made a Mason on sight on January 17, 1936, at the Grand Lodge of the Philippines. Retired from active service in December of 1937, he was recalled to active duty as Lieutenant General and named Commander United States Army Forces in the Far East in July of 1941. In December of that year he was promoted to temporary General, and he led the American forces in various Pacific campaigns between 1941 and 1945. In December of 1944 MacArthur was promoted to temporary General of the Army and received the Medal of Honor for defense preparations and operations in the Philippines. In January of 1945 he was appointed Supreme Allied Commander, Japan, and his rank as General of the Army became permanent. In 1947 he was designated Commander in Chief, Far East Command. Following North Korea's invasion of South Korea, MacArthur was designated Commander, United Nations Command in the Far East in July of 1950.

President Harry S. Truman's removal of General Douglas MacArthur from command of the U.S. Forces in Korea became the most famous civilian-military confrontation in the history of the United States. MacArthur's firing set off a brief uproar among the American public, but Truman held steadfast to his commitment to keep the conflict in Korea from spreading.

General MacArthur was a flamboyant and egotistical man, and problems had been brewing for quite some time. In the early days of the war in Korea (which began in June of 1950), the general had devised brilliant strategies and military maneuvers that helped save South Korea from falling to the invading forces of communist North Korea. As the tide of battle turned in favor of the United States and the United Nations forces MacArthur pushed for advancing into North Korea to completely defeat the communist armies. Truman went along with this plan, but was worried that the communist government of the People's Republic of China might view the invasion as a hostile act and intervene in the conflict. In October of 1950, MacArthur met with Truman and assured him that the chances of a Chinese intervention were slim. Then, between November and December of 1950, hundreds of thousands of Chinese troops crossed into North Korea and drove the American troops back into South Korea. This prompted MacArthur to ask for permission to bomb communist China and use Nationalist Chinese forces from Taiwan against the People's Republic of China. Truman flatly refused these requests, and a very public argument ensued between the two men.

In April of 1951 President Truman fired MacArthur and replaced him with General Matthew Ridgway. On April 11 Truman addressed the nation and explained his actions. He began by defending his overall policy in Korea, declaring, "It is right for us to be in Korea." He criticized the "communists in the Kremlin" of being engaged in a "monstrous conspiracy to stamp out freedom all over the world." Nevertheless, he explained that it "would be wrong; tragically wrong for us to take the initiative of extending the war… Our aim is to avoid the spread of the conflict." Truman further stated, "I believe that we must try to limit the war to Korea for these vital reasons: to make sure that the precious lives of our fighting men are not wasted; to see that the security of our country and the free world is not needlessly jeopardized; and to prevent a third world war." General MacArthur had been fired "so that there would be no doubt or confusion as to the real purpose and aim of our policy."[77]

MacArthur was welcomed back as a hero in the United States. Parades were held in his honor, and he was asked to speak before Congress where he gave his famous "Old soldiers never die, they just fade away" speech. Public opinion was strongly against Truman's actions, but the president stuck to his decision without regret or apology. Eventually, MacArthur did just fade away, and the American people began to understand that his policies and recommendations might have led to a vastly expanded war in Asia.

At the time of MacArthur's removal, President Harry S. Truman was also a Past Grand Master of the Grand Lodge of Missouri. Before dismissing General MacArthur, President Truman consulted with his advisors, including Generals George C. Marshall, who was Secretary of Defense at the time and Omar N. Bradley, who was Chairman of the Joint Chiefs of Staff. In December of 1941 George Marshall had been made a Mason at sight by the Grand Master of the Grand Lodge of the District of Columbia. Omar Bradley had been raised to the third degree in West Point Lodge No.877, Highland Falls, New York in 1923. Dean Atcheson and Averell Harriman were also consulted. The

---

[77] "April 11, 1951: report to the American People on Korea." Miller Center. 26 April 2017. Millercenter.org/the-presidential-speeches/April-11-1951-report-american-people-korea.

recommendation to dismiss General MacArthur was unanimous. Lieutenant General Matthew B. Ridgway who was chosen to relieve MacArthur; he was also a Freemason. Like Bradley, he was a member of West Point Lodge No. 877 and was raised on May 1, 1924.

Freemasonry Returns

As Masonic activities resumed in post-war Japan, the Imperial Household Agency and other top leaders were briefed by Murayama Tamotsu (not yet a Mason) on the fundamental principles of Freemasonry which were to build character and future citizenship.

Prince Higashikuni Naruhiko (uncle of the emperor and Japan's 43rd Prime Minister) showed an interest in becoming a Freemason and was the first Japanese in post-war Japan to present an application to the fraternity. Prince Imperial Yeong (whose wife was a cousin of the empress), Sato Naotake (President of the House of Councillors), Takahashi Ryutaro (Minister of the Ministry of International Trade and Industry), Prime Minister Hatoyama Ichiro (35th and 36th Prime Minister of Japan who served two terms from 1945 to 1956), Kawai Yahachi (President of the House of Councillors), Viscount Mishima Michiharu (a former member of the House of Peers), and many other leaders were among the first group of Japanese citizens to petition the Masonic Order in early 1950.

The question of allowing Japanese to become Freemasons was brought to the Grand Lodge of the Philippines' attention in 1949. They left the decision up to the individual lodges in Japan. Some American Masons opposed the idea based on religious grounds. They argued that the

Japanese candidates should be Christians.

On April 5, 1950, the first group of Japanese were raised to the third degree and made Master Masons. Komatsu Takasho became the first Japanese to occupy the position of Worshipful Master of a Masonic lodge at Tokyo Masonic Lodge No. 125, F. & A. M. (Free and Accepted Masons).[78]

Almost immediately after Murayama Tamotsu's raising, he took the initiative to translate the Masonic rituals into Japanese. By 1954 an all-Japanese degree team (a group of Masons who perform the degrees on candidates) had been assembled and was headed by Lieutenant General Prince Imperial Yeong. He was the 28th Head of the Korean Imperial House, an Imperial Japanese Army general, and the last crown prince of Korea.

Born in Seoul in 1897, he was taken to Japan in December of 1907 and enrolled at Gakushuin Peers' School. The move was meant to ensure that the Korean royal family would not take any further anti-Japanese actions following The Hague Emissary Affair. The Hague Emissary Affair was an incident where Korean Emperor Gojong sent three secret emissaries to the Second Hague Peace Convention (June 15 to October 18, 1907) to declare the invalidity of Japanese diplomatic maneuvers and to assert the monarch's rights to rule Korea independent of Japanese oversight. The emissaries were unable to gain entry into the

---

[78] Wangelin, Tim. "Freemasonry and Modern Japanese History." Freemasonry and Modern Japanese History.
http://www.skirret.com/papers/freemasonry_and_modern_japanese_history.html.

xli. General Douglas MacArthur with Dan Bracken Jr. July 9, 1951

xlii. President Truman wearing his Masonic regalia

xliii. Prince Higashikuni Naruhiko

convention hall as Korea was no longer viewed as an independent nation.

Emperor Meiji, who largely ignored his own grandchildren, devoted a lot of attention to Yeong, acting as his guardian. Upon graduating from Gakushuin, Yeong entered the Imperial Japanese Army Academy in Tokyo. Graduating from the academy on May 25, 1917, he was commissioned a second Lieutenant in the infantry on December 25, and steadily rose up the ranks, receiving promotions to Lieutenant (April 1920), Captain (July 1923), and to Major (August 1928). In 1920, he married Princess Masako of Nashimoto, the eldest daughter of H.I.H. Lieutenant-General Prince Nashimoto Morimasa.

On March 26, 1955, Hatoyama Ichiro and Kawai Yahachi, both Entered Apprentices (first degree Masons), were made Fellowcrafts (second degree Masons) and raised to Master Masons. The second and third degrees were conferred on Hatoyama Ichiro in his home due to his physical condition. Kawai Yahachi's degrees were conferred on him in the Tokyo Masonic Temple. A tea party was held in celebration and many congratulatory messages were read from other Grand Lodges, General MacArthur, and Former President Truman.

xliv. Prince Imperial Yeong

xlv. Sato Naotake circa 1940

xlvi. Hatoyama Ichiro

xlvii. Viscount Mishima Michiharu

The Grand Lodge of Japan was formed in 1957; the charter was granted by the Grand Lodge of the Philippines. The first Japanese Grand Master of the Grand Lodge of Japan was Horiuchi Sadaichi, who served from 1959-1960.[79]

The Grand Lodge of Japan today consists of 15 lodges, four of which are English speaking, eight are bilingual (English and Japanese), and three are strictly Japanese speaking. These lodges are Torri Masonic Lodge No. 6, Nagoya; Tokyo Yuai Lodge No. 11, Tokyo; and Kyoto Mikado Lodge No. 23, Higashiyama-ku, Kyoto.[80]

Other bodies of Freemasons also exist in Japan, as in other countries, such as the Tokyo Scottish Rite bodies, Tokyo York Rite bodies, and the Torii Oasis Shrine Clubs of Japan, which includes the Kanto, Kanagawa, and Misawa Shrine Clubs. The Order of the Eastern Star, an organization for women which is associated with Freemasonry, also exists in Japan.[81] Prince Yeong's wife was initiated into the Eastern Star in 1953. Youth Groups are also present in Japan, such as DeMolay (for boys aged 12-21) and The International Order of the Rainbow (for girls aged 11-20).

The Grand Lodge of Japan, owned by the Masonic Foundation of Japan (formerly the Tokyo Masonic Association) is headquartered in

---

[79] The Official Website of Grand Lodge Japan. www.grandlodgeofjapan.org/pgm.html.
[80] The Official Website of Grand Lodge Japan.
[81] Easternstar.org.www.easternstar.org/joining-order-of-the-eastern-star/.

xlviii. Horiuchi Sadaichi

Tokyo in the Tokyo Masonic Building. It was dedicated in 1981, and it is one of the most modern Masonic temples in the world. All Masonic organizations in Japan have access to the building. The Tokyo Masonic Building is located on the site of the former Japanese Imperial Naval Officers Club. General MacArthur oversaw several Masonic projects including the negotiations with the Japanese government to purchase that land.

CHAPTER 7

Attempts to Suppress Freemasonry

Although Freemasonry spread rapidly and successfully around the globe, countless attempts were made over the years to stop, suppress, and discredit the brotherhood. Following the founding of modern speculative Freemasonry in England in 1717, several governing bodies came to view it as a potential source of opposition.[82] This was due to the secretive nature of the organization and the international connections it had formed. Beginning in 1735 countries such as the Netherlands, Sweden, and Switzerland banned Masonic lodges. Spain, Portugal, France, and Italy followed suit and attempted to suppress Freemasonry after 1738. They were joined by Austria in 1795 and Russia in 1822.

In 1826 the disappearance of William Morgan resulted in increased suspicion of Freemasonry and the formation of the Anti-Masonic Party in the United States.

---

[82] "Founding of the Grand Lodge of England in 1717." Masonicsourcebook.com.

xlix. *Drawing of William Morgan*

William Morgan was born in Culpepper County, Virginia, on August 7, 1774. After his marriage in 1819 and the subsequent birth of his children, Morgan moved his family to York, Upper Canada, where he claimed to have been made a Master Mason. After his business in Canada was destroyed by fire, Morgan returned to the United States, settling first in Rochester, New York, and later in Batavia, where he worked as a bricklayer and stonecutter. He attempted to help establish or visit lodges and chapters in Batavia but was denied participation by members who disapproved of his character and even questioned his claims to Masonic membership. This angered Morgan, who vowed to get even. He announced that he was given a sizable advance by a local newspaper publisher, David Cade Miller, to publish an exposé titled *Illustrations of Masonry*, revealing the secret degree work of the Freemasons in detail. David Miller was said to have received the Entered Apprentice degree (the first degree of Freemasonry) but was prevented from advancing by the Batavia lodge members.

In response to Morgan's threat, several members of the Batavia lodge published an advertisement denouncing him. On September 11, 1826, Morgan was arrested for nonpayment of a loan and allegedly stealing a shirt and a tie. He was jailed in Canandaigua in Ontario County, New York and was to be held there until the loan was repaid. When Miller learned of Morgan's plight, he paid the debt and secured Morgan's release. From there, the two men boarded a waiting carriage that arrived in Fort Niagara the next day. Morgan was neither seen nor heard from afterwards.

In October of 1827, a badly decomposed body washed up on the shores of Lake Ontario. Many presumed it was the body of William Morgan, and the body was buried as his. However, the wife of a missing Canadian man named Timothy Monroe later came forward and positively identified the clothing on the body as that which had belonged to her husband at the time of his disappearance.

A group of Freemasons came forward and claimed that they paid Morgan $500 to leave the country. Morgan was reportedly spotted later in the United States as well as other countries, but none of the reports were actually confirmed. Eventually, Eli Bruce, the sheriff of Niagara County and a Mason, was removed from office and tried for his involvement in Morgan's disappearance. He was convicted of conspiracy for his role in kidnapping Morgan and holding him against his will before his disappearance. The sheriff was therefore sentenced to serve 28 months in prison. Three other Masons, Loton Lawon, Nicholas Chesebro, and Edward Sawyer were convicted of taking part in the kidnapping and served sentences. Other Masons from Batavia were tried and acquitted. DeWitt Clinton, the sixth Governor of New York and a Mason, offered a $1,000 reward for information about Morgan's whereabouts. The money was never claimed.

The allegations surrounding Morgan's disappearance and presumed death sparked a public outcry and protests against Freemasons. Taking advantage of the situation, a New York politician named Thurlow Weed and others founded the new Anti-Masonic Party in opposition to President Andrew Jackson's Democratic Party. Other Jackson rivals including John Quincy Adams joined in denouncing the Masons.

Several states passed laws regulating and restricting Freemasonry that resulted in many cases being brought to court. Anti-Masonic legislation was passed in Vermont in 1833 that included a provision making the giving and taking of an unnecessary oath a crime. (Public Statutes, sec. 5917). The state of New York enacted a Benevolent Orders Law to regulate organizations such as the Freemasons.

The Anti-Masonic Party selected William Wirt as their presidential candidate and Amos Ellmaker as his running mate in the 1832 election.

William Wirt was an American author and statesman who also holds the distinction of being the longest serving Attorney General in United States history. Wirt was a former Freemason who had taken the first two degrees of Freemasonry in Jerusalem Lodge #54 in Richmond, Virginia. Despite his nomination by the Anti-Masonic Party he refused to actively campaign for office and publicly speak out against Freemasonry. In essence, Wirt was perhaps the most reluctant and unwilling presidential candidate ever nominated by an American political party. In his acceptance letter to the nominating convention Wirt stated that he found Freemasonry unobjectionable, and that in his experience "Many Masons were intelligent men of high and honorable character who would never choose Freemasonry above their duties to their God and country."

Amos Ellmaker was a politician, attorney, and judge from Pennsylvania.

The party ticket of Wirt and Ellmaker garnered 7.8 percent of the national popular vote and won the state of Vermont, but Andrew

Jackson easily won the national election. Ellmaker sought election to the United States Senate in 1834, but was defeated by James Buchannan. After the election Amos Ellmaker retired from politics and practiced law in Lancaster, Pennsylvania.

1. Portrait of Andrew Jackson in Masonic regalia as Grand Master

li. *Thurlow Weed*

lii. William Wirt

By 1835 support for the Anti-Masonic Party had declined everywhere but Pennsylvania, as other issues such as slavery had become the focus of national attention.

Millard Fillmore, the 13th President of the United States who had dispatched Commodore Matthew C. Perry on an expedition to Japan with the intent to force the country open for foreign trade initially belonged to the Anti-Masonic Party. In 1932 Fillmore was elected to the House of Representatives as an Anti-Masonic Party candidate.

Many Anti-Masons were opposed to Andrew Jackson's presidential candidacy in 1932 as he was a Freemason. Fillmore was a delegate to the New York convention that endorsed President John Quincy Adams for re-election.

In 1834 Thurlow Weed, Millard Fillmore, and others realized that opposition to Freemasonry was not a strong enough foundation on which to build a national party. They formed the broader-based Whig Party from the National Republicans, Anti-Masons, and dissatisfied Democrats. In 1848 Fillmore was elected the nation's 12th vice president as the Whig Party candidate. He subsequently assumed the role of President following the sudden and unexpected death of President Zachary Taylor.

Soon after Morgan's disappearance, Miller published Morgan's book, which became a bestseller due to the notoriety of the events surrounding his disappearance. Miller never said that Morgan had been murdered but that he had simply been "carried away." Further, it was determined that the handful of Masons who were involved acted on their own accord, and their actions were not sanctioned by the Batavia Lodge.

Having faced difficulties in the United States, Freemasonry also came under attack in all of the Communist countries. Freemasonry was outlawed in the Soviet Union during the Communist era and suppressed by the totalitarian governments of Central Europe (Hungary and Czechoslovakia). The organization managed to survive in Cuba however, and allegedly provided safe haven for dissidents of the Communist regime.

In 1924 Benito Mussolini decreed that all members of his Fascist Party who were Masons must abandon Freemasonry or be barred from the party. In 1925 he dissolved Freemasonry in Italy, claiming that it was a political organization. One of the most prominent Fascists, General Luigi Cappello, who had also been the Deputy Grand Master of the Grande Oriente, gave up his membership in the Fascist Party in favor of his Masonic membership. He was later arrested on false charges and sentenced to 30 years in jail.

In 1919, when Béla Kun declared the dictatorship of the proletariat in Hungary, all Masonic properties were confiscated and placed under public ownership. After the fall of the dictatorship the leaders of the counter-revolution blamed the Hungarian Freemasons for the revolution and also for their World War I defeat. As a result, Freemasonry was outlawed by a decree in 1920, and raids by army officers on Masonic lodges ensued, along with theft and occasional

liii. General Luigi Cappello

destruction of Masonic libraries, records, archives, paraphernalia, and works of art. Several Masonic buildings were seized and used for anti-Masonic exhibitions.

Masonic lodges were re-established in post war Hungary only to be banned again in 1950 after the government declared them to be "meeting places of the enemies of the people's democratic republic, of capitalistic elements, and of the adherents of Western imperialism."[83]

The Nazis alleged that high-degree Masons were willing members of the Jewish conspiracy and Freemasonry was one of the causes for Germany's defeat in World War I.

Jews were first admitted into the brotherhood in the mid-eighteenth century in England. A Jewish lodge, the Lodge of Israel, was established in London in 1793. Later, some lodges in the Netherlands, France, and Germany also allowed Jews to become members. Most German lodges and their members affiliated with the three grand lodges located in Prussia, known collectively as the "Old Prussian Grand Lodges." These grand lodges and their subordinate lodges excluded non-Christians from membership. By 1922, they accounted for 70 percent of all Masons in Germany. Other grand lodges in Germany were known as "humanitarian" lodges since they accepted Jewish and Muslim males as well as Christians. In 1928 the humanitarian lodges had 24,000 members, of which approximately 3,000 were Jews.

---

[83] Jeffers, H. Paul. *Freemasons: A History and Exploration of the World's Oldest Secret Society.* Kensington Publishing Corporation. 2006. P. 163.

Hence, the right wing, conservative political leaders in Europe began to link Jews with Freemasons in the 18th century. Conservatives and Catholic clerics initially painted the Freemasons as hostile to religion and to the accepted aristocratic and clerical order. Since Masonic lodges were generally located in the larger cities of Western Europe and England, where the majority of Western European Jews lived, the link between Jews and Freemasons was further cemented by a rural distrust of the urbanites.

Adolf Hitler, in his 1925 autobiographical book, *Mein Kampf*, wrote, "To strengthen his political position he [the Jew] tries to tear down the racial and civil barriers which for a time continue to restrain him at every step. To this end he fights with all the tenacity innate in him for religious tolerance—and in Freemasonry, which has succumbed to him completely, he has an excellent instrument with which to fight for his aims and put them across. The governing circles and the higher strata of the political and economic bourgeoisie are brought into his nets by the strings of Freemasonry, and never need to suspect what is happening."

In 1933 Hermann Göring, the Reichstag President and one of the key figures in the process of Gleichschaltung ("synchronization"), stated that "In National Socialist Germany, there is no place for Freemasonry."

The Ermächtigungsgesetz (The Enabling Act) passed on March 23, 1933, provided the tool whereby the German Ministry of the Interior ordered the disbandment of Freemasonry on January 8, 1934. The property of all lodges was confiscated and Masons were prohibited from holding office in the Nazi Party or its paramilitary arms. Special sections of the Security Service (SD) and later the Reich Security Main Office (RSHA) were established to deal with Freemasonry. Masons were sent to concentration camps as political prisoners and forced to wear an inverted red triangle on their prison uniforms.

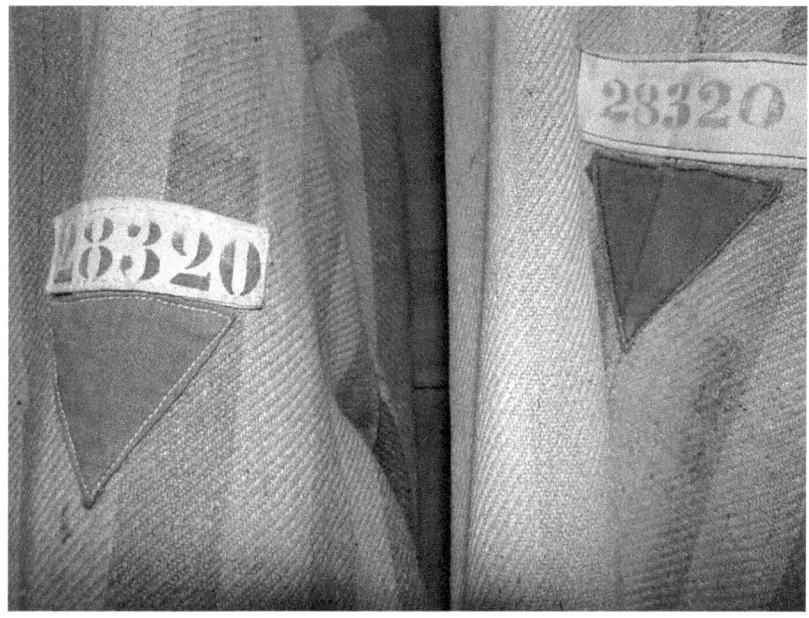

liv. Prisoners' Uniforms with Red Triangles assigned to Political Prisoners - Museum Exhibit - Dachau Concentration Camp Site - Dachau - Bavaria - Germany

During the war, Freemasonry was banned by edict in all countries that were either allied with the Nazis or under Nazi control, including Norway and France. Anti-Masonic exhibitions were held in many occupied countries. Field-Marshal Friedrich Paulus was denounced as a "High-grade Freemason" when he surrendered to the Soviet Union in 1943.

lv. Friedrich Wilhelm Ernst Paulus (June 1942)

In 1943, the anti-Masonic propaganda film *Forces Occultes* was produced in Nazi-occupied France, accusing the Freemasons of conspiring with Jews and Anglo-American nations to incite France into a war with Germany.

The preserved records of the *Reichssicherheitshauptamt* (RSHA), which assisted the SS in the pursuit of their racial objectives through the Race and Resettlement Office, documented the persecution of Freemasons. The actual number of Freemasons from Nazi occupied countries who were killed is not accurately known, but it is estimated that between eighty thousand and two hundred thousand Freemasons were murdered under the Nazi regime.

In Spain, in September of 1928, under the dictatorship of Miguel Primo de Rivera, one of the two grand lodges was closed, and approximately two-hundred Masons, most notably the Grand Master of the Grand Orient, were imprisoned for allegedly plotting against the government.

Following the military coup of 1936, many Freemasons trapped in areas under Nationalist control were arrested and swiftly killed along with left wing party members and trade unionists. It was reported that Freemasons were tortured, strangled, shot, and murdered by organized death squads in practically every town in Spain.

At this time, one of the most fervent opponents of Freemasonry, Father Juan Tusquets Terrats, began to work for the Nationalists with the task of exposing Freemasons. Over the course of two years, he along with Franco's personal chaplain compiled an index of 80,000 suspected

Masons even though there were little more than 5,000 Masons in Spain at the time.

The results were horrific. Countless crimes were committed against Freemasons. In Salamanca, for instance, thirty members of one lodge were shot, including a priest. Freemasons in Lugo, Zamora, Cadiz, and Granada were brutally rounded up and shot, and in Seville the entire membership of several lodges were barbarically butchered. The slightest suspicion of being a Mason was often enough to earn a place before a firing squad. The bloodshed became very intense, and there were grisly stories of Masons being thrown into the working engines of steam trains. By December 16, 1937, according to the annual Masonic Assembly held in Madrid, all Freemasons who had not escaped from the areas under Nationalist control had been murdered.

Following General Francisco Franco's victory, Freemasonry was officially outlawed in Spain. Being a Mason was automatically punishable by a minimum jail term of 12 years.

According to Franco's supporters the Republican Regime which he overthrew had a strong Masonic presence. In reality, Spanish Masons were present in all sectors of politics and the armed forces. At least four of the generals who supported Franco's rebellion were Masons.

After Franco's decree outlawing Freemasonry, Masons were given two months to resign from any lodge where they might have been a member. Many chose to go into exile instead, including prominent monarchists who had whole-heartedly supported the Nationalist rebellion in 1936. The Law for the Repression of Freemasonry and Communism was revoked in 1963.

After the condemnation of Freemasonry by Pope Clement XII in 1738 Sultan Mahmud I outlawed the organization, and since that time Freemasonry has been equated with atheism in the Ottoman Empire and the broader Islamic world.

On July 15, 1978, the Islamic Jurisdictional College, one of the most influential entities that interpret Islamic law issued an opinion that deemed Freemasonry to be "dangerous" and "clandestine."

After World War I, while under the British Mandate, Iraq was home to several lodges. This all changed with the July 14th, 1958 revolution, which abolished the Hashemite Monarchy and resulted in Iraq's transformation into a republic. The licenses permitting lodges to meet were rescinded; later, laws were introduced banning any further meetings. This position was reinforced under Saddam Hussein and the death penalty was "prescribed" for those who "promote or acclaim Zionist principles, including Freemasonry, or who associate [themselves] with Zionist organizations."

Freemasonry is illegal in all Arab/ Islamic countries except Lebanon, Morocco, and Turkey. The Grand Lodge of Turkey (Hür ve Kabul Edilmiş Masonlar Büyük Locası) is the largest of several Masonic grand lodges overseeing Freemasonry in Turkey. It was founded in 1948 and consists of 180 lodges in cities around Turkey. As of 2001 it had an estimated 12,000 members. It is recognized by most grand lodges and follows the traditional Anglo-American style of Freemasonry.

lvi. Hür ve Kabul Edilmiş Masonlar Büyük Locası in Turkey

CHAPTER 8

Freemasons versus Shriners

To the outside world Freemasonry is rather perplexing. This misunderstanding is further compounded by the confusion surrounding the Freemasons and the Shriners. Many believe that the two organizations are the same when in fact they are two very distinct establishments. Founded in 1872, Shriners International is an organization built on the principles which guide Freemasonry, but it also incorporates an element of fun and philanthropy. While all Shriners are Masons, not all Masons are Shriners. Also, there is an aspect of secrecy to Freemasonry which Shriners are not bound to.

Freemasons are required to learn about their fraternity and earn a series of Masonic degrees. When a Mason has completed the third and final degree he becomes a Master Mason and is then eligible to become a Shriner. The rites of the Shrine are styled after Arabic themes and imagery; the Shriners are characterized by their distinctive fez which denotes their membership in a manner similar to the Freemason's apron.

The fez is customized for each member and contains important information about its wearer. The emblem on the front of the fez consists of a crescent and scimitar. The scimitar represents the members, the backbone of the fraternity. The sphinx denotes the governing body for all Shriners. The five-pointed star signifies the children aided by the fraternity's philanthropic efforts. Each fez will also include markings which pertain to membership in Shrine clubs and special roles within the organization. A Shriner may own more than one fez depending on his activities and memberships.

lvii. *Agila Shriner's fez*

Shriners North America, as it was originally known, came into existence in 1870. It was founded by Walter M. Fleming and William J. Florence.

Doctor Walter Millard Fleming was a prominent physician and surgeon who obtained his degree in medicine in Albany, New York, in 1862. He served with the 13th New York Infantry during the Civil War as the brigade's surgeon. Doctor Fleming joined the Masonic fraternity on February 13, 1869, and was raised in Rochester Lodge No. 660.

William Jermyn Conlin, better known by his stage name William J. Florence, was an actor, songwriter, and playwright. It is said that the actor was fond of Florence, Italy, where he kept an apartment and adopted the city's name for his stage name. Florence was initiated into the Mount Moriah Lodge, No. 155 in 1853. He was raised to a thirty-second degree Mason in New York on April 21, 1867.

In 1870 several Masons were attending a luncheon at the Knickerbocker Cottage in Manhattan where the discussion turned to creating a new fraternity stressing fun and fellowship. Fleming and Florence were among the group and they took the idea seriously enough to act upon it.[84]

---

[84] History of the Shrine. Kerakshrine.com/about/history-of-the-shrine.

lviii. Doctor Walter Millard Fleming

lix. William Jermyn Conlin

Florence, while on tour in Marseille, had attended a party hosted by an Arabian diplomat. There he witnessed an elaborately staged musical comedy as part of which the guests became members of a secret society. It is said that Florence took copious notes and made several drawings, which he presented to Fleming when he returned to New York.

Utilizing Florence's notes and sketches, Fleming crafted the rituals, emblem, and costumes for the society. Florence and Fleming launched the fraternity on August 13, 1870 and initiated eleven other members on June 16, 1871. The group embraced the Middle Eastern theme and established the first temple, called Mecca Temple, in New York on September 26, 1872, with Fleming as the first Potentate.

By 1875 the number of Shriners had grown to 43. In an effort to boost membership, the Imperial Grand Council of the Ancient Order of the Nobles of the Mystic Shrine for North America was created on June 6, 1876, with Fleming as the first Imperial Potentate. The move proved successful and by 1878 there were 425 Shriners with 13 temples in 8 states. By 1888 that number increased to 7,210 members with 48 temples dispersed throughout the United States and Canada. From that point Shriner membership grew exponentially. There were 55,000 members and 82 temples in 1900. Shriners International experienced one of its largest growth periods in the years following World War II as returning soldiers looked for new ways to continue the camaraderie they had experienced with their fellow soldiers. Today there are approximately 400,000 members and 200 temples in the United States, Canada, Brazil, Bolivia, Mexico, Panama, the Philippines, Puerto

Rico, Europe, and Australia.

Despite embracing a Middle Eastern theme, the Shriners are in no way connected to the Arab culture nor Islam. The fraternity's only religious requirement is an indirect one; all Shriners must be Masons and petitioners to Freemasonry must profess a belief in a Supreme Being.

The early temples/ shrine centers were often constructed using the Moorish Revival or Neo-Moorish style of architecture. The most notable of these are:

1. The Shrine Auditorium (Los Angeles),
2. The Mecca Temple, currently known as the New York City Center,
3. Newark Symphony Hall,
4. The Mosque, currently known as the Landmark Theater (Richmond, Virginia),
5. The Tripoli Shrine Temple (Milwaukee, Wisconsin),
6. The El Zaribah Shrine Auditorium, currently known as the Polly Rosenbaum Building (Phoenix),
7. The Algeria Shrine Temple, currently known as the Helena Civic Center (Montana),
8. Abou Ben Adhem Shrine Mosque (Springfield, Missouri),
9. The Fox Theatre (Atlanta, Georgia).

The Shriners have an international governing body known as the Imperial Divan. The Imperial Divan functions as a corporate Board of Directors and consists of 12 officers. Each officer is elected to the lowest position on the Divan and moves up one position each year, with the exception of the Imperial Treasurer and the Imperial Recorder.

The Imperial Potentate represents the highest leadership position within Shriners International. The Imperial Potentate is both the president and the CEO of Shriners International. His term is limited to one year and he spends his year in office visiting many of the Shrine temples, attending regional meetings, and visiting the various Shriners Hospitals for Children. He also serves as Chairman of the Board of Directors for both Shriners Hospitals for Children and Shriners International. A similar organizational structure is followed at the local level within each temple/ shrine center.

As a philanthropic organization, the Shriners are dedicated to community service and have been instrumental in countless public projects within their respective territories. Their charitable arm is the Shriners Hospitals for Children, a network of twenty-two hospitals throughout the United States, Mexico, and Canada. The hospitals admit any child under the age of 18 regardless of race, religion, or relationship to a Shriner. Until June of 2012 all care at Shriners Hospitals was provided free of charge. However, due to substantial losses in the stock market, the Shriner's endowment was negatively impacted and the hospitals started billing patients' insurance companies. Free care is still offered to children without insurance, and out of pocket costs that insurance programs do not cover are waived. Also, the Shriners cover all transportation charges for the children and their families whether it is a basic van ride or airline tickets.

In the spirit of fun, the Shriners participate in several local parades. The parade units which are characterized by the use of miniature cars are used to promote a positive image for the fraternity. They also host an annual college all-star football game called the East-West Shrine Game.

The Shriners once hosted a PGA Tour golf tournament in Las Vegas in association with singer, Justin Timberlake, called the Justin Timberlake Shriners Hospitals for Children Open. However, due to Timberlake's lack of participation, this association ended in July of 2012. Despite this, the Shriner's continued to sponsor the PGA Tour tournament through 2017, which was titled The Shriners Hospitals for Children Open.

Many shrine centers also hold an annual Shrine Circus as a fundraiser. The circus was founded in 1906 and travels to approximately 120 cities in the United States. There is a separate unit in Canada which covers 40 cities.

The first Shrine Circus was held in Detroit, Michigan and was originally a one-ring event. By 1925 the circus had grown to three rings. The Detroit circus is still the largest and most attended; however, the most famous venue to host the circus is the Shrine Auditorium in Los Angeles, California.

Like the Freemasons, the Shriners also have their women's auxiliary units. The Ladies' Oriental Shrine and the Daughters of the Nile both support the Shriners Hospitals and promote sociability. Membership in these auxiliary units is open to any woman 18 years of age and older who is related to a Shriner or Master Mason by birth, marriage, or adoption.

The Ladies Oriental Shrine of North America was founded in 1903 in Wheeling, West Virginia, and the Daughters of the Nile was founded in 1913 in Seattle, Washington.

Glossary of Masonic Terms

Appendant Degrees — Lateral movements (honorary degrees) within the highest degree of Master Mason (Third Degree) in the Masonic Rite.

Craft — Originally the word was applied to trades and occupations calling for trained skill. The beginning of Freemasonry is attributed to the skilled stone masons. As Freemasonry transitioned from the Operational Mason to the Speculative (Gentleman) Mason, the term evolved to mean the training one who seeks membership in to the fraternity receives in the form of initiation ceremonies.

Deacons — One of the offices common to all Masonic jurisdictions. In most jurisdictions, a lodge has two Deacons, styled Senior Deacon and Junior Deacon.

The principal duties of the Senior Deacon are to conduct candidates around the lodge and speak for them during certain ceremonies, to attend to the Worshipful Master as needed and to carry his orders to the Senior Warden.

The duties of the Junior Deacon are similar in

many respects to that of the Senior Deacon. In some jurisdictions he is also responsible for guarding the inside of the main door of the lodge.

Degree The steps (from lower to higher) in the progress of a candidate toward the consummation of his membership. (i.e., The Ancient and Accepted Scottish Rite is a system of 33 degrees. The York Rite employs 32 degrees.)

Entered Apprentice One of the three degrees of the Masonic Rite (Entry Level).

Fellowcraft One of the three degrees of the Masonic Rite (The next level above Entered Apprentice).

Grand Lodge The governing body that supervises and governs the individual lodges of Freemasons in any particular geographical area or jurisdiction, (usually corresponding to a national boundary or other major political unit).

Grand Master A title of honor as well as an office in Freemasonry, given to a Mason elected to oversee a Masonic jurisdiction. He presides over a Grand Lodge, and has certain rights in the constituent lodges that form his jurisdiction.

Ineffable Degrees	Appendant Degrees within the Scottish Rite which refer to unspeakable, or unutterable knowledge.
Junior Warden	One of the offices common to all Masonic jurisdictions. The Junior Warden is charged with the supervision of the lodge while it is in recess for meals or other social purposes. In some jurisdictions the Junior Warden has a particular responsibility for ensuring that visiting Masons are in possession of the necessary credentials.
Lodge	The basic organizational unit of Freemasonry. Originally employed by the Operative Masons to mean their building, the group of members or an assembly of Masons. In modern terms, it is a place where Masons meet.
Mother Lodge	The lodge which sponsors the creation of a new lodge, to be warranted under the jurisdiction of the same Grand Lodge. In England, it also identifies the particular lodge where the individual was first made a Mason.
Master Mason	One of the three degrees of the Masonic Rite (Highest Degree attainable). Master was a conventional title applied to persons in superior

rank. In Freemasonry, it denotes the person who has proven himself capable of mastering the work or belonging to a Degree so named. (The Order's Third Degree.)

Operative Mason A person who was engaged in the skilled trade of stone masonry.

Past Master At the conclusion of his limited term of office, a Worshipful Master is termed a Past Master. The duties and privileges of Past Masters vary from lodge to lodge and jurisdiction to jurisdiction.

Provincial Grand Lodge Provincial Grand Lodges are administrative subdivisions of a Grand Lodge.

Provincial Grand Master Provincial Grand Master (abbreviated PGM or PrGM), sometimes called District Grand Master or Metropolitan Grand Master, is a fraternal office held by the head of a Provincial Grand Lodge, who is directly appointed by the organization's Grand Master.

Rites A series of progressive degrees that are conferred by various Masonic organizations or bodies, each of which operates under the control of its own central authority:

Ancient and Primitive Rite
Emulation Rite
English Rite
French Rite
National Mexican Rite
Primitive Scottish Rite
Rectified Scottish Rite
Rite of Adoption
Rite of Baldwyn
Rite of Memphis-Misraim
Rite of Strict Observance
Scottish Rite
Schröder Rite
Swedish Rite
York Rite (also known as "American Rite")

Secretary One of the offices common to all Masonic jurisdictions. The Secretary's official duties include issuing the summons (a formal notice of an impending meeting, with time, date and agenda), recording meeting minutes, completing statistical returns to the Grand Lodge, and advising the Worshipful Master on matters of procedure.

Senior Warden One of the offices common to all Masonic jurisdictions. The Senior Warden (sometimes known as First Warden) is the second of the three principal officers of a lodge, and is the Master's principal deputy. Under some constitutions, if the Worshipful Master is absent, the Senior Warden presides at meetings as "acting Master," and may act for the Master in all matters of lodge business.

Speculative (Gentleman) Mason   The basis for today's Masonic membership. Similar to the Operative Masons who trained specifically as skilled stone workers, the Speculative Mason is trained to improve to improve his life as well as the lives of others.

Stewards   One of the offices common to all Masonic jurisdictions. Stewards fulfill a number of junior assistant roles. There is some variance, even within the same jurisdiction, as to the precise roles played by Stewards. Some of their common duties could include the following:

> *Stewards are often tasked with an understudy role to fill the position of the Senior Deacon or Junior Deacon, in their absence.*

> *When a degree ceremony is performed, one or more Steward(s) may be required to assist the two Deacons in conducting the candidates*

around the temple.

Stewards have a traditional role in many jurisdictions of serving wine at any meal after the lodge meeting, often extended to a general supervision and planning of catering and refreshments.

Supreme Council	The governing body of Scottish Rite Freemasonry in its jurisdiction.
Treasurer	One of the offices common to all Masonic jurisdictions. The role of the Treasurer is to keep the accounts, collect annual dues from the members, pay bills, and forward annual dues to the Grand Lodge.
Tyler	One of the offices common to all Masonic jurisdictions. He is sometimes known as the *Outer Guard* of the lodge. His duty is to guard the door (from the outside), with a drawn sword, and ensure that only those who are duly qualified gain entry into the lodge meeting. In some jurisdictions, he also prepares candidates for their admission.

The Tyler is traditionally responsible for preparing the lodge room before the meeting, and for storing and maintaining the regalia after the meeting.

Worshipful Master The senior officer of a Masonic lodge. The office of Worshipful Master is the highest honor to which a lodge may appoint any of its members.

LIST OF PHOTOS AND ILLUSTRATIONS

i. *Alle Frimurer Symboler* (Illustration from Masonic Emblems published by George Kenning, London, Liverpool and Glasgow, April 1874), Public domain. — 3

ii. *Statue of George Washington in Masonic garb at the Masonic Hall in New York City*, By Rhododendrites via Wikimedia Commons (Creative Commons Attribution-Share Alike 4.0 International). — 10

iii. *Benjamin Franklin Opening the Lodge* (Published by Kurz and Allison of Chicago, 1896), Public domain. — 11

iv. *Pythagorean tetractys* (https://commons.wikimedia.org/wiki/File:Tetractys.svg), Public domain. — 13

v. *The Eye of Providence as seen on the U.S. $1 bill* (https://en.wikipedia.org/wiki/Eye_of_Providence#/media/File:Dollarnote_siegel_hq.jpg), via Wikimedia Commons, Public domain. — 15

vi. *Masonic Third Degree Tracing Board showing Hiram Abiff in his coffin*, By unknown artist (Circa 1830s) from the Museum of Freemasonry, Public domain. — 18

vii. *The Knights Hospitaller in the 13th century*, By Ralph Hammann, Wikimedia Commons, (CC BY-SA 4.0). — 20

viii. *A piece of jewelry of the "18° Knight of the Rose Croix" Scottish Rite -20th century image*, By Cro-maat via Wikimedia Commons (CC BY-SA 3.0). — 22

ix. *Freemasonry emblem -the masonic square and compass symbol*, Juliia Kryszhevska via Dreamstime.com (Royalty free stock photo). 24

x. *Prince Augustus Frederick, Duke of Sussex* (1773-1843) via Wikimedia Commons, Public domain. 37

xi. *Mother Lodge building in Kilwinning, North Ayrshire, Scotland*, By Secondarywaltz via Wikimedia Commons (CC BY-SA 4.0). 39

xii. *GODF - The Grand Temple, the largest conference and meeting room where several lodges occasionally meet*, Public domain. 44

xiii. *Minutes from the founding of Große National-Mutterloge, Zu den drei Weltkugeln*, via Wikimedia Commons, Public domain. 45

xiv. *Ivan Perfilievich Yelagin (1725–94)*, via Wikimedia Commons, Public domain. 47

xv. *Portrait of Prince Hall* (c.1735 – December 4, 1807), via Wikimedia Commons, Public domain. 49

xvi. *Confucius* (Portrait by Qiu Ying (1494–1552), via Wikimedia Commons, Public domain. 56

xvii. *Laozi* By Shelipe via Wikimedia Commons (Creative Commons Attribution-Share Alike 4.0 International). 57

xviii. *William Chalmers, Director of the Swedish East India Company and a Freemason*, via Wikimedia Commons, Public domain.   62

xix. *Prince Gong*, via Wikimedia Commons, Public domain.   66

xx. *Dr. Sun Yat-sen pictured (seated, second from right) with the Chicago branch of the Tongmenghui in 1911.* By Huang Wing Shingao via Wikimedia Commons (CC BY-SA 4.0).   69

xxi. *Dr. Sun Yat-sen (seated) and Chiang Kai-shek* via Wikimedia Commons, Public domain.   70

xxii. *Tokyo, 1900 (from left) Suenage Takashi, Uchida Ryohei, Miyazaki Torazo, Koyama Yutaro, Kiyofuji Koshichiro, and Sun Yat-sen* via Wikimedia Commons, Public domain.   75

xxiii. *Situ Meitang* via Wikimedia Commons, Public domain.   77

xxiv. *The China Zhi Gong Party* via Wikimedia Commons, Public domain.   79

xxv. *Franklin D. Roosevelt designated in the photograph as a 32nd degree Freemason* via Franklin D. Roosevelt Presidential Library and Museum, Public domain.   80

xxvi. *Puyi in 1961, flanked by Xiong Bingkun, a commander in the Wuchang Uprising, and Lu Zhonglin, who took part in Puyi's expulsion from the Forbidden City in 1924* via Wikimedia Commons, Public domain.   83

xxvii. *Members of the Chinese Freemasons, Vernon, British Columbia, 1926*, Public domain.   85

xxviii. *Umbrella Revolution, umbrellas in Causeway Bay (Photo by Doctor Ho)* via Wikimedia Common (Creative Commons Attribution-Share Alike 2.0 Generic).   92

xxix. *Viscount Tadasu Hayashi (1850 – 1913) in circa 1902* via Wikimedia Commons, Public domain.   97

xxx. *Commodore Matthew Calbraith Perry* By Matthew Brady – This image is available from the United States Library of Congress's Prints and Photographs division under the digital ID cph.3g07502, Public domain.   109

xxxi. *Sakamoto Ryoma* via Wikimedia Commons, Public domain.   111

xxxii. *Thomas Blake Glover, recipient of the Order of the Rising Sun* via Wikimedia Commons, Public domain.   114

xxxiii. *Glover with Iwasaki Yanosuke, the brother of the founder of Mitsubishi, circa 1900* via Wikimedia Commons, Public domain.   115

xxxiv. *The Choshu Five in 1863* via Wikimedia Commons, Public domain.   117

xxxv. *Glover House known as Ipponmatsu (Single Pine Tree) from a drawing of 1863. The tree was chopped down in the early 1900s* via Wikimedia Foundation, Public domain.   118

xxxvi. *Gate of the former Nagasaki Lodge No. 710 located in Glover Garden* via Wikimedia Commons, Public domain.   119

xxxviii. *J.R. Black* via Wikimedia Commons, Public domain.   124

xxxix. *Nishi Amane* By Takahashi Yuichi 1893 via Wikimedia Commons, Public domain.   125

xl. *Tsuda Mamichi* via Wikimedia Commons, Public domain.   129

xli. *Murayama Tamotsu* (Center), Public domain.   136

xlii. *General Douglas MacArthur with Dan Bracken Jr.* July 9, 1951, International news photos, Public domain.   142

xliii. *President Truman wearing his Masonic regalia*, Abbie Rowe, National Park Service, Harry S. Truman Library & Museum, Public domain.   143

xliv. *Prince Higashikuni Naruhiko* via Wikimedia Commons, Public domain.   144

xlv. *Prince Imperial Yeong* via Wikimedia Commons, Public domain.   146

xlvi. *Sato Naotake circa 1940* via Wikimedia Commons, Public domain.   147

xlvii. *Hatoyama Ichiro*, Inuyo Cabinet Compilation, Inuyo Cabinet (1932) via Wikimedia Commons, Public domain.   148

xlviii. *Viscount Mishima Michiharu* 13 May 1953 via Wikimedia Commons, Public domain.   149 xlix. *Horiuchi Sadaichi* (Grand Lodge of Japan) via Wikimedia Commons, Public domain.   151

l. *Drawing of William Morgan,* A. Cooley - The Grand Lodge of British Columbia and Yukon via Wikimedia Commons, Public domain.   153

li. *Portrait of Andrew Jackson in Masonic regalia as Grand Master*, Washington Bogart Cooper - Grand Lodge of Tennessee via Wikimedia Commons, Public domain.   157

lii. *Thurlow Weed*, Library of Congress Prints and Photographs Division. Brady-Handy Photograph Collection. http://hdl.loc.gov/loc.pnp/cwpbh.01230. via Wikimedia Commons, Public domain.   158

liii. *William Wirt*, this image is available from the United States Library of Congress's Prints and Photographsdivision (https://www.loc.gov/rr/print/) under the digital ID cph.3b37500 (http://hdl.loc.gov/loc.pnp/cph.3b37500) via Wikimedia Commons, Public domain.   159

liv. *General Luigi Cappello*, 1918 o prima, Vent'anni di storia via Wikimedia Commons, Public domain.   162

lv. *Prisoners' Uniforms with Red Triangles assigned to Political Prisoners* - Museum Exhibit - Dachau Concentration Camp Site - Dachau - Bavaria – Germany By Adam Jones, Ph.D. via Wikimedia Commons (Creative Commons Attribution-Share Alike 3.0 Unported).   165

lvi. *Friedrich Wilhelm Ernst Paulus* (June 1942), this image was provided to Wikimedia Commons by the German Federal Archive (http://www.bundesarchiv.de/) (Deutsches Bundesarchiv) as part of a cooperation project, via Wikimedia Commons (Creative Commons Attribution-Share Alike 3.0 Germany).   166

lvii. *Hür ve Kabul Edilmiş Masonlar Büyük Locası in Turkey* By Hevesli via Wikimedia Commons (Creative Commons Attribution-Share Alike 3.0 Unported).   170

lviii. *Agila Shriner's fez* By Rojear20 via Wikimedia Commons, (Creative Commons Attribution-Share Alike 3.0 Unported).   172

lix. *Doctor Walter Millard Fleming*, source: http://www.araratshrine.com/history/famous/img/fleming/walterfleming_dr200.jpg via Wikimedia Commons, Public domain.   174

lx. *William Jermyn Conlin* , source: Matthews, Brander and Hutton, Laurence , eds. (1900). Actors and Actresses of Great Britain and the UnitedStates, Vol. 5: Edwin Booth and His Contemporaries, https://books.google.com/books?id=waIVAAAAYAAJ&) NewIllustrated Edition. L.C. Page & Co., Boston, after p. 114 via Wikimedia Commons, Public domain (the copyright has expired because its first publication occurred prior to January 1, 1927).   175

WORKS CITED

"2014 Hong Kong protests." Wikipedia. Wikimedia Foundation. https://en.wikipedia.org/wiki/2014_Hong_Kong_protests.

Addison II, L.C. "The Tenets of Freemasonry: Mere Words or Good Guidelines?" Grand Lodge of Iowa.org. http://grandlodgeofiowa.org/docs/Philosophy_Masonry/TheTenetsOfFreemasonry.pdf.

"Æthelstan." Wikipedia. Wikimedia Foundation. https://en.wikipedia.org/wiki/%C3%86thelstan.

"Antient Grand Lodge of England." Wikipedia. Wikimedia Foundation. https://en.wikipedia.org/wiki/Antient_Grand_Lodge_of_England.

"April 11, 1951: report to the American People on Korea." Miller Center. 26 April 2017. Millercenter.org/the-presidential-speeches/April-11-1951-report-american-people-korea.

"Arai Hakuseki." Wikipedia. Wikimedia Foundation. https://en.wikipedia.org/wiki/Arai_Hakuseki.

Bessel, Paul M. "Bigotry and the Murder of Freemasonry." Constitution. November 1994. Bessel.org/naziart.htm.

"Bushido." Wikipedia. Wikimedia Foundation. https://en.wikipedia.org/wiki/Bushido.

Calder, John Fulton." Meiji-era Portraits. http://meiji-portraits.de/meiji_c.html#CALDERJohnFulton.

"Canton System." Encyclopædia Britannica. Encyclopædia Britannica, Inc. https://www.britannica.com/event/Canton-system.

Cartwright, Mark. "Knights Hospitaller." World History Encyclopedia. https://www.worldhistory.org/Knights_Hospitaller/.

"China Zhi Gong Party." Wikipedia. Wikimedia Foundation. https://en.wikipedia.org/China_Zhi_Gong_Party.

Cozens, Ken. "Swedes, Merchants, Freemasons and East India Company Agents in 18th Century East London." Port Towns and Urban Cultures. https://porttowns.port.ac.uk/swedes-merchants/.

"Definition of tenet." Merriam-Webster Online. https://www.merriam-webster.com/dictionary/tenet.

Easternstar.org.www.easternstar.org/joining-order-of-the-eastern-star/.

"The Equilateral Triangle." The Grand Lodge of Texas. The Masonic Trowel.com. http://www.themasonictrowel.com/Articles/degrees/degree_3rd_files/theequilateral_triangle_gltx.htm.

"Founding of the Grand Lodge of England in 1717." Masonicsourcebook.com.

"Freemasons." In Roosevelt History. https://fdrlibrary.wordpress.com/tag/freemasons/.

"Freemasonry in China." Zetland Hall. https://zetlandhall.com/history/china.

"Freemasonry in Mexico." Wikipedia. Wikimedia Foundation. https://en.wikipedia.org/wiki/Freemasonry_in_Mexico.

"Freemasonry of Massachusetts." Paul Revere Lodge of Freemasons. https://paulreverlodge.org.

"Furen Literary Society." Wikipedia. Wikimedia Foundation. https://en.wikipedia.org/wiki/Furen_Literary_Society.
"Gormogons." Wikipedia. Wikimedia Foundation. https://en.wikipedia.org/wiki/Gormogons

"Grand National Mother Lodge, "The Three Globes"." Wikipedia. Wikimedia Foundation. https://en.wikipedia.org/wiki/Grand_National_Mother_Lodge,%22The_Three_Globes%22.

"Grand Orient De France." Wikipedia. Wikimedia Foundation. https://en.wikipedia.org/wiki/Grand_Orient_de_France.

"Grand Orient of Italy." Wikipedia. Wikimedia Foundation. https://en.wikipedia.org/wiki/Grand_Orient_of_Italy.

"Greco-Roman Mysteries." Wikipedia. Wikimedia Foundation. https://en.wikipedia.org/wiki/Greco-Roman_mysteries.

"Grill Family." Wikipedia. Wikimedia Foundation. https://en.wikipedia.org/wiki/Grill_family.

"Guan Yu." Wikipedia. Wikimedia Foundation. https://en.wikipedia.org/wiki/Guan_Yu.

"Guide to Shinto Shrines in Japan - Features and Styles." Guide to Shinto Shrines in Japan - Features and Styles | Asia Highlights. https://www.asiahighlights.com/japan/guide-to-shinto-shrines.

"Hayashi Razan." Wikipedia. Wikimedia Foundation. https;//en.wikipedia.org/wiki/Hayashi_Razan.

"Hermetic Order of the Golden Dawn." Wikipedia. Wikimedia Foundation. https://en.wikipedia.org/wiki/Hermetic_Order_of_the_Golden_Dawn.

"Hiram Abiff." Wikipedia. Wikimedia Foundation. https://en.wikipedia.org/wiki/Hiram_Abiff.

History.com Editors. "Meiji Restoration." History.com, A&E Television Networks. https://www.history.com/topics/japan/meiji-restoration#:~:text=at%20the%20center.-,Edo%20Period%3A%20Economy%20and%20Society,four%20classes%20was%20officially%20prohibited.

"History of Freemasonry in Russia." Wikipedia. Wikimedia Foundation.
https://en.wikipedia.org/wiki/History_of_Freemasonry_in_Russia.

"History of Jardine Matheson & Co.." Wikipedia. Wikimedia Foundation.
https://en.wikipedia.org/wiki/History_of_Jardine_Matheson_%26_Co.

"History of Freemasonry." Masonic Service Association of North America. http://www.msana.com/historyfm.asp.

"History of Freemasonry." Wikipedia. Wikimedia Foundation.
https://en.wikipedia.org/wiki/History_of_Freemasonry.
History of the Shrine. Kerakshrine.com/about/history-of-the-shrine.

"Hongmen: The Chinese Freemason's history stretches back to mid-seventeenth century secret societies in Southern China." Grand Lodge of British Columbia and Yukon.
http://freemasonry.bcy.ca/history/chinese_freemasons/index.html.

"Jean Abraham Grill." Wikipedia. Wikimedia Foundation. https://en.wikipedia.org/wiki/Jean_Abraham_Grill.

Jeffers, H. Paul. Freemasons: A History and Exploration of the World's Oldest Secret Society. Kensington Publishing Corporation. 2006.

"Kilwinning Abbey." Wikipedia. Wikimedia Foundation. https://en.wikipedia.org/wiki/Kilwinning_Abbey.

"Knights Templar Discoveries." KnoghtsTemplarFreemasonry.com. http://www.knightstemplarfreemasonry.com/temlar_freemasonry_connection.htm.

Koninck, Christian. (1978) "The Maritime Routes of the Swedish East India Company During Its First and Second Charter (1731-1766)." Taylor and Frances Online. www.tandfonline.com/doi/abs/10.1080/03583322.1978.10407895.

"Masonic Manuscripts." Wikipedia. Wikimedia Foundation. https://en.wikipedia.org/wiki/Masonic_manuscripts.

Mathews, John T. "The Candidate." Masonic Relief, Charity and You. Masonic World. www.masonicworld.com/education/files/artnov01/The%20Candidate.htm.

Murray, Dian H. and Baoqi, Qin. The Origins of the Tiandhui: The Chinese Triads in Legend and History. Standford University Press. July 1, 1994.

"Mystery religion: Greco-Roman religion." Encyclopedia Britannica. https://www.britannica.com/topic/mystery-religion.

Neo-Confucianism." Wikipedia. Wikimedia Foundation. https://en.wikipedia.org/wiki/Neo-Confucianism.

The Official Website of Grand Lodge Japan. www.grandlodgeofjapan.org/pgm.html.

"Opium Wars." Encyclopædia Britannica. Encyclopædia Britannica, Inc. https://www.britannica.com/topic/Opium-Wars.

"Premier Grand Lodge of England." Wikipedia. Wikimedia Foundation. https://en.wikipedia.org/wiki/Premier_Grand_Lodge_of_England.

"Proto-Indo-Iranian religion." Wikipedia. Wikimedia Foundation. https://en.wikipedia.org/wiki/Proto-Indo-Iranian_religion.

"Rosicrucianism." TheosophyWiki. http://theosophy.wiki/w-en/index.php?title=Rosicrucianism.

"Rosicrucianism." Wikipedia. Wikimedia Foundation. https://en.wikipedia.org/wiki/Rosicrucianism.

"Secular Mystery Communities." Encyclopædia Britannica, Encyclopædia Britannica, Inc., https://www.britannica.com/topic/mystery-religion/Secular-mystery-communities.

"Silk Road." Encyclopædia Britannica. Encyclopædia Britannica, Inc. https://www.britannica.com/topic/Silk-Road-trade-route.

(Situ Meitang)维基媒体项目贡献者. "司徒美堂." 维基百科，自由的百科全, Wikimedia Foundation, Inc. https://zh-m-wikipedia-org.translate.goog/zh-hans/%E5%8F%B8%E5%BE%92%E7%BE%8E%E5%A0%82?_x_tr_sl=zh-CN&_x_tr_tl=en&_x_tr_hl=en&_x_tr_pto=sc.

"Square and Compasses." Wikipedia. Wikimedia Foundation. https://en.wikipedia.org/wiki/Square_and_Compasses.

"Sun Yat-Sen." Wikipedia. Wikimedia Foundation. https://en.wikipedia.org/wiki/Sun_Yat-sen.

"Swedish East India Company." Wikipedia. Wikimedia Foundation. https://en.wikipedia.org/wiki/Swedish_East_India_Company.

"Taoism and Confucianism - Ancient Philosophies." Ushistory.org, Independence Hall Association.
https://www.ushistory.org/civ/9e.asp.

"Tetractys." Wikipedia. Wikimedia Foundation. https://en.wikipedia.org/wiki/Tetractys

"Toten Miyazaki." Wikipedia. Wikimedia Foundation. https://en.wikipedia.org/wiki/T%C5%8Dten_Miyazaki.

"Thomas Smith Webb." Wikipedia. Wikimedia Foundation. https://en.wikipedia.org/wiki/Thomas_Smith_Webb.

"Tiandihui." Wikipedia. Wikimedia Foundation. https://en.wikipedia.org/wiki/Tiandihui.

"Thomas Glover." 三菱グループサイト, https://www.mitsubishi.com/en/profile/history/series/thomas/.

"Umbrella Movement." Wikiedia. Wikimedia Foundation. https://en.wikipedia.org/wiki/Umbrella_Movement.

"United Grand Lodge of England." Wikipedia. Wikimedia Foundation. https://en.wikipedia.org/wiki/United_Grand_Lodge_of_England.

"Vol. 6 Yataro & Ryoma-Sharing a Common Dream." Mitsubishi Corporation. www.mitsubishicorp.com/jp/en/mclibrary/roots/vol06/.

Wangelin, Tim. "Freemasonry and Modern Japanese History." Freemasonry and Modern Japanese History.

http://www.skirret.com/papers/freemasonry_and_modern_japanese_history.html.

"Welcome to UGLE, 2018." United Grand Lodge of England. www.ugle.org.uk/about-freemasonry/frequently-asked-questions.

"Who Are the Freemason?" Be a Shriner Now. www.beashrinernow.com/About/Freemasons/AboutFreemasons.

"William Chalmers (merchant)." Wikipedia. Wikimedia Foundation. https://en.wikipedia.ord/wiki/William_Chalmers_(merchant).

"William Shaw." Wikipedia. Wikimedia Foundation. https://en.wikipedia.org/wiki/William_Schaw.

"Who Built the Pyramids?" Nova. http://www.pbs.org/wgbh/nova/ancient/who-built-the-pyramids.html

Wing Lo, T. "Securitizing the Colour Revolution: Assessing the Political Role of Triads in Hong Kong's Umbrella Movement ." Academic.oup.com. https://academic.oup.com/bjc/article/61/6/1521/6261040.

"World Civilizations II (HIS102) – Biel." From the Edo Period to Meiji Restoration in Japan | World Civilizations II (HIS102) – Biel, https://courses.lumenlearning.com/suny-fmccworldcivilization2/chapter/from-the-edo-period-to-meiji-restoration-in-japan/.

"Zerubbabel." Wikipedia. Wikimedia Foundation. https://en.wikipedia.org/wiki/Zerubbabel.

ABOUT THE AUTHOR

KRISTINE OHKUBO is a Los Angeles-based author and editor whose work emphasizes topics related to Japan and Japanese culture. While growing up in Chicago, she developed a deep love and appreciation for Japanese culture, people, and history. Her extensive travels in Japan have enabled her to gain insight into this fascinating country, which she shares with you through her work.

Her first book, a travel guide to Japan, was published in 2016. In 2017, she released a historical study of the Pacific War written from the perspective of the Japanese people, both those who were living in Japan and in the United States, when the war broke out. Two years later, she supplemented her earlier releases with the story of an infamous twentieth century geisha, who was both a victim and an aggressor, struggling amidst a strict patriarchal culture and a rapidly changing social system. In 2019, she followed up her 2017 release, *The Sun Will Rise Again*, with a book titled *Sakhalin*. The work examines the far-reaching impact the island changing hands had on its inhabitants and resources and culminates with the tragic events which took place in August 1945.

Beginning in 2020, Kristine turned her attention to rakugo, Japan's 400-year-old art of storytelling. She released two books, *Talking About Rakugo 1: the Japanese Art of Storytelling* followed by *Talking About Rakugo 2: The Stories Behind the Storytellers*. Through a succession of biographical information, anecdotes, interviews, and rakugo scripts, the author explains why this traditional art form has endured for many years.

In 2022, Kristine contributed her editing skills to yet another rakugo book, this one authored by English rakugo storyteller Kanariya Eiraku entitled *Eiraku's 100 English Rakugo Scripts (Volume 1)*. Following its release in August of the same year, she revisited a work she had first published three years earlier.

Originally released in January 2019, *Asia's Masonic Reformation: Freemasonry's Impact on the Westernization and Subsequent Modernization of Asia* examines how Freemasons have historically been the catalysts for change throughout Asia and the rest of the world. Utilizing careful research and setting aside the misinformation and various conspiracy theories that have emerged throughout the decades, the revised second edition presents the details and irrefutable historical facts demonstrating how Freemasons have notably been at the forefront, ushering in rapid change, modernization, and enlightenment.

As an author, Kristine believes that writing from other cultural perspectives encourages empathy and understanding, and at the same time it broadens our knowledge of the events that have unfolded over the years.

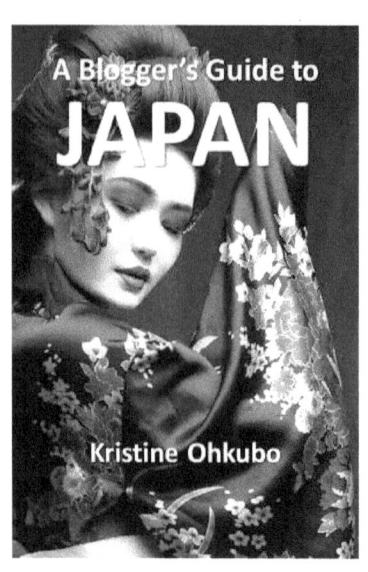

A Blogger's Guide to Japan

Published : November 23, 2016
Language : English
Paperback : 476 pages
ISBN-10 : 1539033112
ISBN-13 : 978-1539033110

The Sun Will Rise Again

Published : October 31, 2017
Language : English
Paperback : 230 pages
ISBN-10 : 1540747956
ISBN-13 : 978-1540747952

Nickname Flower of Evil (呼び名は悪の花): The Abe Sada Story

Published : September 17, 2019
Language : English
Paperback : 162 pages
ISBN-10 : 0578551470
ISBN-13 : 978-0578551470

Sakhalin: The Island of Unspoken Struggles

Published : September 28, 2020
Language : English
Paperback : 206 pages
ISBN-10 : 1087902983
ISBN-13 : 978-1087902982

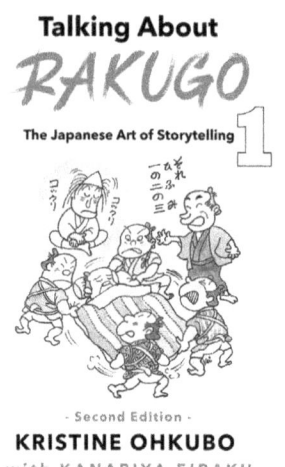

Talking About Rakugo 1: The Japanese Art of Storytelling

Published : April 14, 2022 (2nd ed.)
Language : English
Paperback : 474 pages
ISBN-10 : 1088023606
ISBN-13 : 978-1088023600

Talking About Rakugo 2: The Stories Behind the Storytellers

Published : February 7, 2022
Language : English
Paperback : 298 pages
ISBN-10 : 1087984599
ISBN-13 : 978-1087984599

Eiraku's 100 English Rakugo Scripts (Volume 1)
(*Edited by Kristine Ohkubo*)

Published : August 17, 2022
Language : English
Paperback : 350 pages
ISBN-10 : 1088061680
ISBN-13 : 978-1088061688

www.ingramcontent.com/pod-product-compliance
Lightning Source LLC
Chambersburg PA
CBHW062033290426
44109CB00026B/2614